Minnesota Writes:
Poetry

MINNESOTA WRITES: POETRY

Edited by Jim Moore and Cary Waterman

Sponsored by The Loft
MILKWEED EDITIONS/NODIN PRESS

© 1987 by Milkweed Editions and Nodin Press
All rights reserved. Published 1987.
Published in the United States of America

90 89 88 87   4 3 2 1

Published by Milkweed Editions and Nodin Press
Books may be ordered from the address below:
Post Office Box 3226
Minneapolis, Minnesota 55403

Edited by Jim Moore and Cary Waterman
Design and Cover Illustration © R.W. Scholes

ISBN 0-915943-21-2

This publication is supported in part by a grant
provided by the Literature Program of the National
Endowment for the Arts, by the First Bank Systems
Foundation, and by the Arts Development Fund of
United Arts with Special Assistance from the McKnight
Foundation.

Acknowledgements

We gratefully acknowledge permission to reprint materials from the following sources:

DANIEL BACHHUBER, "Snowstorm," *Milkweed Chronicle*, Volume 6, Number 1, Winter, 1985, © by the author. Reprinted by permission of the author.

ROBERT BLY, "Awakening" and "After Drinking All Night with a Friend, We Go Out in a Boat to See Who Can Write the Best Poem." From *Silence in the Snowy Fields* (Wesleyan University Press, 1962) © by the author. Reprinted by permission of the author. "The Dead Seal" and "The Hockey Poem." From *The Morning Glory* (Harper and Row, 1975), © by the author. Reprinted by permission of the author. "A Dream of Retarded Children." From *This Tree Will Be Here for A Thousand Years* (Harper and Row, 1979), © by the author. Reprinted by permission of Harper and Row. "Counting Small Boned Bodies" and "When the Dead Speak." From *The Light Around the Body* (Harper and Row, 1967), © by the author. Reprinted by permission of Harper and Row. "For My Son Noah" and "My Father's Wedding." From *The Man in the Black Coat Turns* (Doubleday, 1981), © by the author. Reprinted by permission of Doubleday. "In Rainy September" and "Listening to the Köln Concert." From *Loving a Woman in Two Worlds* (Doubleday, 1985), © by the author. Reprinted by permission of Doubleday.

JILL BRECKENRIDGE, "Cabell — Moving from Virginia to Kentucky — Grandmother Shows Me a Letter Sent to Grandfather from Colonel Thompson Who Took Our Slaves to Kentucky and Then Hired Out: June, 1792," "Jacob — The Four Seasons: Harvest," "Will Sommers, Confederate Soldier — December 30, 1862: The Night Before the Battle He Prepares to Fight, Gun Not Loaded," "Tad Preston, Cadet — Quiet now . . . Attack!" and "The South (IV)." From *Civil Blood* (Milkweed Editions, 1986), © by the author. Reprinted by permission of the author.

MICHAEL DENNIS BROWNE, "Talk to Me, Baby," "Fox" and "Bach's Birthday." From *The Sun Fetcher* (Carnegie-Mellon University Press, 1978), © by the author. Reprinted by permission of Carnegie-Mellon Press.

BARRY CASSELMAN, "Psalm of Your Amino Anthems," *Another Chicago Magazine*, 1985, © by the author. Reprinted by permission of the author. "The Gates of Atonement Opening," *Abraxas*, Number 34, 1986, © by the author. Reprinted by permission of

Editors' Prefaces

In 1971, when I first came to Minnesota, there wasn't so much a community of poets as a group of friends and acquaintances who lived throughout the state and whose paths occasionally crossed at poetry readings and other such gatherings.

In 1987 that small group has turned into something much larger, much more diverse. No doubt it is less intimate now, but it is at the same time more open and much more complex. If the appropriate metaphor for 1971 was that of an extended family — with relatives scattered all over the state and the usual squabbles and joys, rituals and traditions, black sheep and patriarchs and matriarchs associated with a family — it is more accurate to speak today of a *community* of poets, hundreds of men and women with a vital interest in the writing and reading of poetry but with few of the close families ties — shared values and assumptions — that united poets here in the early seventies.

Of the fifteen years that I've lived here, this seems to me the most exciting, surprising, and challenging time to be a poet. While the diversity of writing styles has not ossified into schools and diehard cliques (as I understand they have in some other parts of the country), there is a lively and increasingly articulate sense of the different approaches it is possible to take towards poetry. This anthology reflects and celebrates these differing approaches.

After going through the difficult and sometimes harrowing process of making the decisions about whom to include in this anthology, it is utterly clear to me how subjective the process is, how open to question, how haunted by second thoughts an editor must inevitably be.

I had hoped, when I first thought about writing this introductory essay, to find certain common Minnesota — or at least, Midwestern — themes. But other than certain subjects (hockey, for example) which would be less likely to appear in a similar anthology from Florida, there seem to me few, if any, common themes or subjects.

The only exception to this lack of commonality that I can find has to do with something much harder to pin down than subject matter or theme. I can't think of a single word for it, but if you crossed *serious* and *earnest* you would come up with the tone that I mean. Something just this side of lugubriousness, something with an edge to it: *if you don't waste my time. I won't waste yours.*

This seriousness/earnestness, often takes a strangely humorous turn in many of the prose poems included here. Perhaps this form invites—or permits—the poet to loosen up in a way that's more difficult to do in lined poetry. Or perhaps it's partly a function of the new interest in short personal essays—those meeting places between prose and poetry that have always intrigued writers—an interest that has grown here as well as in other regions of the country.

In any case, this is the first comprehensive anthology of Minnesota poetry to appear in many years. While much of the work included responds to Midwestern and specifically Minnesota landscape, a sense of place that is landlocked and interior, it is also a poetry that reflects the realities of what it means to live in the late twentieth century: the regional is instantly linked to the national and the global.

The anthology speaks eloquently to the truth that attention to place is crucial, but that far from creating a poetry of solely regional concerns, such attention draws the poet inevitably into the larger world within which the region must somehow find its place.

—James Moore

The poems in this anthology were selected because of their passion and because of their ability to stay resonating in the mind and heart long after the moment of reading. They are like the small but tough chickadees who come to my feeder on cold winter mornings. These birds are as dependable as the grass which slumbers under a hard crust of snow. The bright, delicious notes of their call linger long after the winter sun has dropped beyond the rim.

Editing this anthology has been both exciting and frustrating. The great diversity of voices in Minnesota is overwhelming. One finally becomes speechless when confronted with so many who work at telling their own particular truth and the truth, also, of their place and their time. And editors are limited, no matter how great the effort, by their own subjectivity which precludes any wish for perfection. It would have been easy to have included here many more poets. Reality, however, dictated selection. In reading and rereading the manuscripts submitted for possible inclusion in this anthology, I found myself reminded more than once of the derogatory statement made years ago by a visiting poet to this state who remarked on the prevalence of "that flat Midwestern diction." I was reminded of this because it is so utterly untrue. Minnesota has been fertile ground for all kinds of poets with their many particular voices.

This is, I believe, a great strength. Notwithstanding all the recent discussion, both for and against that slippery idea of regionalism, I am hard pressed to find among the many poets represented here a commonality which is less than universal. Certainly there is an observation of place, but is this not what all good writers do whether they live in Paris or Minnesota? And merely writing out of a certain locale does not a regionalist make.

This is not the same thing, however, as saying these poems could have been written anywhere. What is true is that these poems and the poets who have written them are not limited by a regional philosophy or diction or subject matter. The whole idea of regionalism is something thought up by a culture dependent on labeling and categorizing. If it can be labeled, it can be controlled; if it can be categorized, it can be manipulated. The poems in this anthology will not sit still for that. They move around, and often in very unexpected directions. It's enough to drive mad the Dictator of Neat and Tidy Divisions.

However, we are here. This is Minnesota. These are Minnesota poets. They write about the snow, but they also write about the many turnings of love. They write about harvests of field corn and about ice-fishing, but they also write of the seasons of loss and the gift of children. And who is to say that in another landscape their art would not repeat these same moral and universal themes? The concern is not so much for the regional as for the real.

There is a photograph in the August 1986 *National Geographic* of rocks along the Rio Pinturas in the Patagonian region of southern Argentina where the Toldenese people, who are believed to have been the earliest inhabitants of the region, sprayed solutions of ocher around their hands, leaving on the rocks white handprints that seem to wave hello to us across the centuries. These "signatures" are seven to nine thousand years old, have withstood time and the elements, and "speak" to us of a fundamental humanity and commonality of all people. Whether we leave a handprint or a poem, each of us will be enriched by this giving and by this receiving.

—Cary Waterman

Contents

JAMES WHITE, 1936–1981, is the author of *The Salt Ecstasies* (Graywolf Press, 1981), and three earlier collections: *Divorce Proceedings, A Crow's Story of Deer* and *Del Rio Hotel*. White edited *Time of the Indian*, an anthology of Indian student writing and *First Skin Around Me*, an anthology of Indian writing from around the country. Before coming to Minnesota, White was the creator and director of the Navajo Folk Art Theatre and for five years worked closely with the Navajo. In Minnesota, he was a director of the Indian Project of the Minnesota Poets in the Schools Program for COMPAS, and also taught at The Loft, A Place for Literature and the Arts, in Minneapolis.

An Ordinary Composure

I question what poetry will tremble the wall into hearing or tilt
the stone angel's slight wings at words of the past like a memory
caught in elms. We see nothing ahead. My people and I lean
against great medical buildings with news of our predicted death,
and give up mostly between one and three in the morning, never
finding space large enough for a true departure, so our eyes gaze
earthward, wanting to say something simple as *the meal's too small:
I want more.* Then we empty from a room on Intensive Care into
the sea, releasing our being into the slap of waves.

Poems break down here at the thought of arms never coupling
into full moons by holding those we love again, and so we resort
to the romantic: a white horse set quivering like a slab of marble
into dancing flesh.

Why remember being around a picnic table over at Brookside
Park? We played softball that afternoon. My mother wore her
sweater even in the summer because of the diabetes. Night black-
ened the lake like a caught breath. We packed things up. I think I
was going to school that fall or a job somewhere. Michael'd go
to Korea. Before we left I hit the torn softball into the lake and
Michael said, 'You can't do that for shit James Lee.'

Going back I realized the picnic was for us. It started raining in a
totally different way, knowing we'd grow right on up into wars
and trains and deaths and loving people and leaving them and
being left and being alone.

That's the way of my life, the ordinary composure of loving,
loneliness and death, and too these prayers at the waves, the
white horse shimmering, bringing it toward us out of coldest
marble.

JAMES WHITE

THOMAS MCGRATH was born in North Dakota. He is the author of *Letter to An Imaginary Friend* (Parts I and II), *The Movie at the End of the World: Collected Poems* (Swallow Press), *Waiting for the Angel* (Uzzano Press, 1979), *Passages Toward the Dark* (Copper Canyon, 1982), *Echoes Inside the Labyrinth* (Thunder's Mouth Press, 1983). Between periods of teaching, McGrath was a free-lance writer of fiction and film, mostly documentary. He has received a Guggenheim Fellowship, 1968–69, a Bush Foundation Fellowship, 1976–77, and 1981–82, and for 1987, an NEA Senior Fellowship for poetry.

McGrath lives in Minneapolis. His son Tom (sometimes Tomasito) is finishing high school.

The Trouble With The Times

for Naomi Replansky

In this town the shops are all the same:
Bread, Bullets, the usual flowers
Are sold but no one — no one, no one
Has a shop for angels,
No one sells orchid bread, no one
A silver bullet to kill a king.

No one in this town has heard
Of fox-fire rosaries — instead
They have catechisms of filthy shirts,
And their god goes by on crutches
In the stench of exhaust fumes and dirty stories.

No one is opening — even on credit —
A shop for the replacement of lost years.
No one sells treasure maps. No one
Retails a poem at so much per love.

No. It is necessary
To go down to the river where the bums at evening
Assemble their histories like cancelled stamps.
There you may find, perhaps, the purple
Weather, for nothing; the blue
Apples, free; the reddest
Antelope coming down to drink at the river,
Given away.

THOMAS MCGRATH

Letter To An Imaginary Friend
Part I Section III

4.

My father took me as far as he could that summer,
Those midnights, mostly, back from his long haul.
But mostly Cal, one of the bundle teamsters,
My sun-blackened Virgil of the spitting circle,
Led me from depth to depth.

                                                  Toward the light
I was too young to enter.
He must have been about thirty. As thin as a post,
As tough as whang-leather, with a brick-topped mulish face,
A quiet talker. He read *The Industrial Worker*,
Though I didn't know what the paper was at the time.
The last of the real Wobs—that, too, I didn't know,
Couldn't.

                                     Played a harmonica; sat after supper
In the lantern smell and late bat-whickering dusk,
Playing mumbly-peg and talked of wages and hours
At the bunkhouse door. On Sunday cleaned his gun,
A Colt .38 that he let me shoot at a hawk—
It jumped in my hand and my whole arm tingled with shock.
A quiet man with the smell of the road on him,
The smell of far places. Romantic as all of the stiffs
Were romantic to me and my cousins,
Stick-in-the-mud burgesses of boyhood's country.

What he tried to teach me was how to take my time,
Not to be impatient, not to shy at the fences,
Not to push on the reins, not to baulk nor pull leather.
Tried to teach me when to laugh and when to be serious,
When to laugh at the serious, be serious in my laughter,
To laugh at myself and be serious with myself.
He wanted me to grow without growing too fast for myself.
A good teacher, a brother.

5.

That was the year, too, of the labor troubles on the rigs—
The first, or the last maybe. I heard the talk.

It was dull. Then, one day—windy—
We were threshing flax I remember, toward the end of the run—
After quarter-time I think—the slant light falling
Into the blackened stubble that shut like a fan toward the
    headland—
The strike started then. Why *then* I don't know.
Cal spoke for the men and my uncle cursed him.
I remember that ugly sound, like some animal cry touching me
Deep and cold, and I ran toward them
And the fighting started.
My uncle punched him. I heard the breaking crunch
Of his teeth going and the blood leaped out of his mouth
Over his neck and shirt—I heard their gruntings and strainings
Like love at night or men working hard together,
And heard the meaty thumpings, like beating a grain sack
As my uncle punched his body—I remember the dust
Jumped from his shirt.
He fell in the blackened stubble
Rose
Was smashed in the face
Stumbled up
Fell
Rose
Lay on his side in the harsh long slanting sun
And the blood ran out of his mouth and onto his shoulder.

Then I heard the quiet and that I was crying—
They had shut down the engine.
                                    The last of the bundle-teams
Was coming in at a gallop.
                                        Crying and cursing
Yelled at the crew: "Can't you jump the son-of-a-bitch!
Cal! Cal! Get up"
But he didn't get up.
None of them moved.
Raging at my uncle I ran.
Got slapped,
Ran sobbing straight to the engine.
I don't know what I intended. To start the thing maybe,

THOMAS MCGRATH

To run her straight down the belt and into the feeder
Like a vast iron bundle.
I jammed the drive-lever over, lashed back on the throttle,
And the drive belt popped and jumped and the thresher groaned,
The beaters clutched at the air, knives flashed,
And I wrestled the clutch.

                             Far away, I heard them
Yelling my name, but it didn't sound like my own,
And the clutch stuck. (Did I want it to stick?) I hammered it
And the fireman came on a run and grabbed me and held me
Sobbing and screaming and fighting, my hand clenched
On the whistle rope while it screamed down all of our noises —
Stampeding a couple of empties into the field —
A long, long blast, hoarse, with the falling, brazen
Melancholy of engines when the pressure's falling.

Quiet then. My uncle was cursing the Reds,
Ordering the rig to start, but no one started.
The men drifted away.

                             The water monkey
Came in with his load.

                                    Questioned.
He got no answer.
Cal's buddy and someone else got him up
On an empty rack and they started out for home,
Him lying on the flat rack-bed.

Still crying, I picked up his hat that lay in the churned up dust,
And left my rack and team and my uncle's threats,
And cut for home across the river quarter.

    6.

Green permission . . .

                        Dusk of the brass whistle . . .
Gooseberry dark.
Green moonlight of willow.
Ironwood, basswood and the horny elm.
June berry; box-elder; thick in the thorny brake
The black choke cherry, the high broken ash and the slick
White bark of poplar.

                              I called the king of the woods,
The wind-sprung oak.
                                      I called the queen of ivy,
Maharani to his rut-barked duchies;
Summoned the foxgrape, the lank woodbine,
And the small flowers: the wood violets, the cold
Spears of the iris, the spikes of the ghostflower—
It was before the alphabet of trees
Or later.
                              Runeless I stood in the green rain
Of the leaves.
                    Waiting.
                            Nothing.
                                    Echo of distant horns.
Then

Under the hush and whisper of the wood,
I heard the echoes of the little war.
A fox barked in the hills; and a red hawk boomed
Down on the darkening flats in a feathery splash of hunger.
Silence and waiting.
                                    The rivery rustle
Of a hunting mink.
                            Upstream in the chuckling shallows
A beaver spanked the water where, in its time,
The dam would be where my brother, now in his diapers,
Would trap for the beaver's grandsons.

                                    I could not
See in that green dark.
                                    I went downstream
Below the crossing where I'd swum the midnight river
On my way home from a move.
                                    I put my clothes,
Stinking with sweat and dusty (I thought:
How the dust had jumped from Cal's shirt!)
                            I put them on the broken stump.

I dived from the hummock where the cut-bank crumbled.

Under the river the silence was humming, singing:
Night-song.

THOMAS MCGRATH

                                        In the arrest and glaucous light
Delicate, snake-like, the water-weed waved and retracted.
The water sang. The blood in my ears whistled.
I roared up out of the river into the last of the sunlight.

Then: I heard the green singing of the leaves;
The water-mystery,
The night-deep and teasing terror on the lone river
Sang in my bones,
And under its eves and seas I broke my weeping,
In that deeper grieving,
The long, halting — the halt and the long hurry —
Toward the heaving, harsh, the green blurring of the salt
     mysterious sea.

     7.

Later, climbing the coulee hills in the sandy dusk,
After sundown in the long northern twilight,
The night hawk circling where the ragamuffin crows
Steered for the cloudy wood;
In that dead calm, in that flat light,
(The water darkening where the cattle stood to their knees)
I heard the singing of the little clan.
Comfort of crickets and a thrum of frogs.
Sleepy rustle of birds.

In the dusk the bats hustled.
The hawk wheeled and whirled on the tall perch of the air;
Whirled, fell
Down a long cliff of light, sliding from day into dusk.
Something squealed in the brake.
The crickets were silent.
The cattle lifted their blank and unregardant
Gaze to the hills.
Then, up the long slope of air on his stony, unwavering wing
The hawk plunged upward into a shower of light.

The crickets sang. The frogs
Were weaving their tweeds in the river shallows.

Hawk swoop.
        Silence.
                Singing.
The formal calls of a round-dance.
This riddling of the river-mystery I could not read.

Then, climbing the high pass of my loss, I tramped
Up the dark coulee.
                The farmyard dark was dappled
With yellowy ponds of light, where the lanterns hung.
It was quiet and empty.
                  In the hot clutter
Of the kitchen my mother was weeping. "He wouldn't eat."
She said, meaning Cal.
              She had a womanly notion
(Which she didn't really believe) that all man's troubles
Could be ended by eating—it was a gesture she made
To soothe the world.
My father had driven my uncle out of the yard
Because Cal was *our* man, and not to be mistreated
Any more than horses or dogs. He was also my father's friend.
I got some supper and took it out to the barn.
In the lemony pale light of a lantern, at the far end,
He lay in a stall. His partner sat in the straw
Beside him, whittling, not looking at me. I didn't ask
Where his gun was, that slept in an oily rag
In his suitcase.
            I put the food beside him
As I'd done with sick dogs.
           He was gone where my love
Nor my partisanship could reach him.

Outside the barn my father knelt in the dust
In the lantern light fixing a harness. Wanting
Just to be around, I suppose, to try to show Cal
He couldn't desert him.
           He held the tubular punch
With its spur-like rowel, punching a worn hame strap
And shook the bright copper rivets out of a box.
"Hard lines, Tom," he said. "Hard lines, Old Timer."

      THOMAS MCGRATH

I sat in the lantern's circle, the world of men,
And heard Cal breathe in his stall.

                                    An army of crickets
Rasped in my ear.

                               "Don't hate anybody,"
My father said.
I went toward the house through the dark.

That night the men all left.

                              Along toward morning
I heard the rattle of Fords. They had left Cal there
In the bloody dust that day but they wouldn't work after that.
"The folded arms of the workers" I heard Warren saying,
Sometime in the future where Mister Peets lies dreaming
Of a universal voting-machine.

                             And Showboat
Quinn goes by (New York, later) "The fuckin' proletariat
Is in love with its fuckin' chains. How do you put this fuckin'
Strike on a cost-plus basis?"

There were strikes on other rigs that day, most of them lost,
And, on the second night, a few barns burned.
After that a scattering of flat alky bottles,
Gasoline filled, were found, buried in bundles.

"The folded arms of the workers."
I see Sodaberg
Organizing the tow boats.

                        I see him on Brooklyn Bridge,
The fizzing dynamite fuse as it drops on the barges.
Then Mac with his mournful face comes round the corner
(New York) up from the blazing waterfront, preaching
His strikes.

             And my neighbors are striking on Marsh Street.
(L.A., and later)

                           And the hawk falls.

A dream-borne singing troubles my still boy's sleep
In the high night where Cal had gone:

                           They came through

The high passes, they crossed the dark mountains
In a month of snow.
Finding the plain, the bitter water, the iron
Rivers of the black north . . .

Hunters
                       in the high plateaus of that country . . .

Climbing toward sleep . . .

But far
                    from the laughter.

THOMAS MCGRATH

Letter To An Imaginary Friend
Part III Section II

I.

. . . too dark to say anything clearly, but not too dark
To see . . .
            one foot in early twilight, the other in snow,
(Now failing away in the western sky where a fair star
Is traveling our half-filled trail from the still, far field—
O rare light!—trailing us home toward the farmhouse lamp)
We go:
     home:
          and then, with a shout!, my brother Jimmy
Leaps! And cleaves to my back on the little sled:
                       and we're home . . .

             ******

But not too dark to see . . .
                 It is snowing in Lisbon,
                       Tomasito!
(At the corner of *Rua do Karma* and Rolling Stone Square
Where I'm living and loning and longing for you.)
                     Portuguese winter!
A snow of leaflets falls from the hot and dumbstruck sky.
Midnight Mass for the Fourth and Fourteenth of July, Tomasito!
Or maybe the snow of Pentecost: the leaflets speak in *all* tongues
Of men and angels—and maybe it's time to change
                 angels . . .
Still . . . *not* too dark to see . . .
               (—was right *here*
Somewheres—place we got lost . . .)
               And I *do* see:
                 here:
                   clearly
(Having third sight) *primero* (and aside from all the political
Palindromes) I see the beautiful girls of the Poor,
(More beautiful than all the nineteen thousand Marys) rusting
Under the hailing and merry slogans of the Tetragrammaton
Of the Revolution

THOMAS McGRATH

                    —each Throne, Counter-throne, Power and
      Dominion
Of the hierarchy of those fallen angels signed with Hammer &
      Sickle!
They rust and rest—or their simulacra of holy pictures—
Where I saw them once before, among the foreign money,
On the back walls of earlier bars and wars . . .
                                        their asses
Widen . . .
            icons . . .
                        calendar queens . . .
                              (And Cal's girl,
                                    too . . .)
Some have wakened to fight in the man-killing streets, but these,
      enchanted,
Dream-chained in the burning palace of Capital, slumber . . .
They sleep where Custer sleeps and only Keogh's horse
Is alive . . .
            over cheap bars where *pão* and *vinho verde*
Have not changed into their bodies of bread and wine . . .
                                              Not
Changed, yet, but changing: for also in those darkbright streets
I can hear the guns (seven, twenty-seven, seventy-five)
Of the July Days . . .
                  (though they haven't started shooting yet).
                                        And the bells
On the trucks of soldiers and armed workers.
                                    But few of the latter—
Alas . . .
        Like the girls, the Workers' Councils (soviets) are resting
Or rusting . . .
              —Though they and the damned poor are
      wrestling for the Body of Good
Through the ten thousand parties of the Revolution:
                                          there
                                    in the
                                    shouting
Streets that all end in the cold sea.
                        No time!

                        —32—   THOMAS MCGRATH

For love!

      (Though this is a kind of love.)

                     It is time! (they sing!)

                              Time!

(And the bells clang from the rushing trucks and the tall towers)
Time! — to change angles and angels and to reinstate
Cham, Amoymon, Marx, Engels, Lenin, Azael,
Stalin, Mahazael, Mao, Sitrael — Che-Kachina —
O yield up the names of the final Tetragrammaton! —
Time! To make sacred what was profane! Time! Time!
Time!

      to angelize the demons and the damned . . .

    2.

And we, of the damned poor, trot our frost-furred horses
Into the barn where beyond the glinting lantern, a blessed
And a steamy animal sleep is clotting into a night
Dreamless, perhaps, or, if blurred by dreams, it is green as
      summer
And the hay that burns there — a cattle-barn night, star lighted
By rays from the deadwhite nailheads shining in their rime-laced
                                  albs.

The yard is corralling the darkness now, but Orient offers
A ghost-pale waning moon host-thin in the wan and failing
Light:
The sun that brief December day now gone
Toward topaz distances . . . of mineral afternoons
Beyond the Bad Lands . . .

                 toward Montana . . .

                        the shandy
                      westernesses . . .

And we three (who are now but one in the changed and
                              changing
Dark of my personal fading and falling world) we three
Hand in hand and hand in heart sail to the house —
My father has lent me the light so we can go hand in hand,
Himself between us, the lantern brighter than any moon!

Indoors, my mother bends over the stove, her face rosy
In the crackling woodfire that winks and spits from an open lid.
And we *all* there, then, as we were, once,
On the planet of sadness in a happy time. (We did not, then,
Miss you, Tomasito, an unsuffered age away
Waiting for all my errors to make me one time right.)

And so I will name them here for the last time, who were once
Upon the earth in a time greener than this:
My next brother Jim, then Joe, then my only sister, Kathleen,
Then Martin, then Jack, the baby.
                                        Now Jim and Jack have gone
Into the dark with my mother and father. But then—
                                                        Oh, then!
How bright their faces shone that lamplit Christmas Eve!
And our mother, her whole being a lamp in all times and
        weather . . .
And our father, the dear flesh-gantry that lifted us all from the
        dark . . .

        [In that transfiguring light, from the kitchen wall, a Christ
        Opens his chest like an album to show us his pierced heart
        As he peers from a church calendar almost empty of days
        Now: say, then, who among you might not open your flesh
        On an album of loss and pain—icons of those you have
                                                        loved
        Gone on without you: forever farther than Montana or
                                                        sundown?
        No Christ ever suffered pain longer or stronger than
                                                        this . . .]

So let me keep them now—and forever—fixed in that lost
Light
        as I take the lantern and go down the stairs to the cellar
In search of the Christmas apples cold in their brimming bin.
There, as deep in the hull of a ship, the silence collects
Till I hear through the dead-calm new-come night the far bells:
Sheldon . . .
                Enderlin . . .
                                bells of the little towns
                                                calling . . .

THOMAS MCGRATH

Lisbon . . . North Dakota . . .
                              [Yes, I hear them now
    In this other time I am walking, this other Lisbon,
                              Portugal—
    Bells of the Revolution, loud as my heart I hear
    Above the continuous bad-rap of the urine-colored sea.
    Beside which I am walking through that snow of July
                              leaflets
    In search of the elusive onion to make the home-done
                              sandwich
    Herbaical and vegetable and no doubt even healthy, and
                              certainly
    Hearty-seeming (in mind's tongue) after fifteen K's and quais
    A la recherche de cebolla perdue:
                    Vegicum Apostolicum
    Herbibable sancti et ecumenicabable . . .
                              Meanwhile
    I die on the vine waiting for news from you, Tomasito,
    Waiting for the angel, waiting for news from heaven, a new
    Heaven, of course—and a better world in birth! *Here*:
    Under the changing leaflets under the flailing bells.]

And the bells of Sheldon carry me up the steep of the stairs,
My feet set in a dance to be bearer of these cold apples,
The fairest fruit of our summer labor and harvest luck.
I lay them out on the lamplit table. On the gleaming cloth,
In the dreamy gaze of the children they glaze in a lake of gold!

O high wake I have said I would hold!
                              It has come all unknown:
Unknown!
          And my blood freezes
                    to see them so:
In *that* light
          in this
                    light
                    each face all-hallowed
In the haloing golden aura shining around each head!

And how black and stark these shadows lean out of the hollow
    dark

To halloo and hold and hail them and nail them into the night
Empty
       —its leaden reaches and its cold passage
                          empty . . .

And so, at that last supper, in the gold and blood of their being,
So let me leave them now and forever fixed in that light.

   3.

To go from Cham to Amoymon!
                    Toward Midnight Mass!
                             And
                           the frost
Filing the iron of the runners or the runners filing the snow!
It sets our teeth on edge, that gritting and steely protest
Against our going. But we go all in joy! In joy
Our holy carols and catcalls collect from the coulee hills
Their coiling and icy answers like echoes drawn from the stars!

         THOMAS MCGRATH

Ode For The American Dead In Asia

1.

God love you now, if no one else will ever,
Corpse in the paddy, or dead on a high hill
In the fine and ruinous summer of a war
You never wanted. All your false flags were
Of bravery and ignorance, like grade school maps:
Colors of countries you would never see—
Until that weekend in eternity
When, laughing, well armed, perfectly ready to kill
The world and your brother, the safe commanders sent
You into your future. Oh, dead on a hill,
Dead in a paddy, leeched and tumbled to
A tomb of footnotes. We mourn a changeling: you:
Handselled to poverty and drummed to war
By distinguished masters whom you never knew.

2.

The bee that spins his metal from the sun,
The shy mole drifting like a miner ghost
Through midnight earth—all happy creatures run
As strict as trains on rails the circuits of
Blind instinct. Happy in your summer follies,
You mined a culture that was mined for war:
The state to mold you, church to bless, and always
The elders to confirm you in your ignorance.
No scholar put your thinking cap on nor
Warned that in dead seas fishes died in schools
Before inventing legs to walk the land.
The rulers stuck a tennis racket in your hand,
An Ark against the flood. In time of change
Courage is not enough: the blind moles dies,
And you on your hill, who did not know the rules.

3.

Wet in the windy counties of the dawn
The lone crow skirls his draggled passage home:
And God (whose sparrows fall aslant his gaze,
Like grace or confetti) blinks and he is gone,

And you are gone. Your scarecrow valor grows
And rusts like early lilac while the rose
Blooms in Dakota and the stock exchange
Flowers. Roses, rents, all things conspire
To crown your death with wreaths of living fire.
And the public mourners come: the politic tear
Is cast in the Forum. But, in another year,
We will mourn you, whose fossil courage fills
The limestone histories: brave: ignorant: amazed:
Dead in the rice paddies, dead on the nameless hills.

THOMAS MCGRATH

KATE GREEN has published two books of poetry, *The Bell in the Silent Body* (Minnesota Writers' Publishing House, 1977) and *If the World Is Running Out* (Holy Cow! Press, 1983). Her first novel, *Shattered Moon* (Dell, 1986) was published in six foreign countries and has been optioned for film rights by United Artists. Her second novel is forthcoming from Dell in the next year. Green has received a Bush Foundation Fellowship for Individual Artists and other awards. She teaches writing at Hamline University in St. Paul and is a member of the adjunct writing faculty at the University of Minnesota.

Green lives in St. Paul with her husband and two sons, Raphael, 6, and Elliot, 4.

Saturday Night At The Emporium Of Jazz

God, if there be a heaven,
let it be Saturday night
at the Emporium of Jazz in Mendota,
Jay McShann in a shimmering brown suit,
his hands blurred reflections
in perfectly sheened ebony
of the piano. Smoke in air
dusky like half-rain
outside November night. Let it be
two hundred miles from the headwaters
of the Mississippi River, let
St. Louis, Kansas City, New Orleans
be in a long line beneath us
in America. And music
come off his big back,
lift off like wings of many birds
on a migratory river, stamping
water-surface flight. And let
three horns stand upright
at stage edge, silver cornet,
black clarinet, golden
tall trombone on the red
indoor-outdoor carpeting
of the low stage,
a fire extinguisher on the floor
next to the piano
for when the music gets hot
and a pile of spilled ice cubes
next to the piano bench
melting in the pink spotlight.
Let there be clink of glasses
and loud voices back by the bar
so you get angry. Dear God,
let heaven be loud, let there be
human anger in a white cloud.
Let music make you forget
the blood in your hands
that can not stop patting
your bended knee and may Jay
McShann's whole body play,

KATE GREEN

not just hands but all ten
fingers a choir on keys
never before touched and then
touched in every way by a man
in a roadhouse bar in this
fog of a dark country. Let love
be this clear and direct, *Baby,*
don't you want a man like me?
Let one glass be half full
of whiskey and the other
full of beer. *Baby, let me*
love you til my face turns cherry red.
Trains cross America in our minds,
pure as old jazz tuned
in broad backs bent to work
on a piece of metal, a hot stove,
back bent over a crib
and back bent over a woman
in an unmade bed out of some longing
that skin can satisfy.
Let that song go out in this heaven,
Jay McShann at the baby grand.
Let earth be small, hot smoke,
full ashtray, dark on one side
of the river, music on the other,
while the last note lingers,
growling,
over the cold, cold water.

Blanche

for my grandmother

She's shrunk now and blue,
the color of smoke or a jelly glass.
We sit drinking Sanka.
"I'm a little fuzzy in the mornings," she says.
"I can't remember things. I need lists:
what day the doctor, hairdresser Tuesday,
milk, aspirin, sherry.
Just two small glasses in the afternoon."

I talk because I'm afraid
to ask how are you,
afraid she'll say she can't remember
or tell me her back is burning.
Her eyes cloud some days so she thinks she's been crying
but can't remember why.
"You know, it's not so bad
here at the residence," she says.
"It's just dull."
Plants on sill in pink foil,
poinsettias still blooming in March
the box room lined with photos of her husband
who died in 1946
and I wonder if she's been touched since
beneath the nylon layers,
powder and sag in the swell under her girdle
or if she ever liked it.

I say, "Let's get down the albums."
We sit side by side on the bed and turn over 80 years,
black pages, gray snow,
the silver her family never found in Colorado.
"Here we are posing," she says.
"This is so old, before the scarlet fever took my hair.
My mother was not a happy woman.

Here's Father, Ephraim, a depot master in Westcliff,
population about 40 and 10 of them were us.
We could ride the train free,
but Mother never went anywhere, just France once.
They shipped over all the mothers of the war dead.

KATE GREEN

She went to Don's grave.
He drowned in a ditch near Avignon
two days after Armistice.
Here she is again.
I always said I never wanted to be a fat old woman like her.
Here's a picnic. Berry picking.
None of the boys came back from the war."

Blanche brushes my arm like a moth,
holds the seven books of descendents,
every name in mind: Arthur, George, Bertha, Edith, Jim, Kate.
"Nell's dead now. *I get fuzzy in the mornings.*"
Eighty years of dinners,
blades poised over the neck of the turkey,
fresh babies propped on women's knees.
Blur: the speed at which Blanche and I fall
dizzy through the century of our births
grabbing fragments of all that is lost.
"Here is Italy! Is it? Is it Rome? Is it Florence?
Where are my glasses? It's all out of order.
Oh my poor brain."

She grows younger, moored to the stuck faces.
"Look, my queer wedding.
Your grandfather Paul on a train.
I guess it all did add up.
So much happened."

Blanche leans back into pillows, her chest concave.
For no apparent reason, she remembers a tiny white coffin
in the parlor upstairs from the train depot
where she lived as a girl.
Perfumed flowers in the dust.
The baby's closed eyelids, blueveined,
lips translucent as insect wings and the hair—

"The hair," she says,
"I wanted to touch it just once.
It was golden. No one was looking.
I stretched out one finger

but there was such a sadness in the house,
I felt I shouldn't touch it.
A sister.
And no one ever spoke of her again.
Imagine.
She could have had a whole life."

KATE GREEN

Baptism

Miles Davis on the stereo and snow falling down between the building, he began to sing, "*How I got over / How I got over / Sometimes I look back and wonder / How I got over.*" And "*There is a balm / In Gilead / That heals the sin sick so-oul / There is a balm / In Gilead / That makes the wounded whole,*" holding the notes out in a tremulous voice while I joined in on harmony, having learned the songs in junior high school choir singing all-white spirituals.

"Did I tell you I was the soloist in the youth choir when I was a kid?" he said. "Oh yeah. In my little blue suit and scared to death, humming in front of the choir while they rocking back and forth real slow in rhythm with the fans. First row was the deaconesses, the way they used to tuck their kleenex in the sleeve of their dress and fan themselves with the program? And out comes me singing, the choir goes huuuuuuuummmmmmm and holds it out long and I go, *Jesus all right / Jesus all right*' and they echo, *He's all right / He's all right.*' Then me: *He's a doctor and a lawyer / He heal the sick and He feed the poor / When you strung out on dope / And you know you can't cope / When you ain't got a dime/ And you doing some time / He'll be right there with you / And His angels too.*' YEAH," said Burt.

"Then there was the day I got baptized. You been baptized?" he said.
"When I was seven. At the Episcopal Church. My grandmother made my mother do it. I forced my mother to buy me an Easter hat."
"But did you get dunked all the way under?"
"No, they just stuck my face in a birdbath."
"Then you ain't been baptized." he said. "Sometime I'm going to do it to you."
"What are you, a minister or something?"
"A New Age Black Baptist Evolutionary Transcendental Minister from the Church of the Violet Ray," he grinned. "All my people been ministers, my grandfather, I got an uncle in L.A. — he used be a shark, man, running numbers, two-bit crook from Tulsa. He had a hole drilled in his front tooth and a diamond inlaid. For real. One day he had a vision of the Holy Spirit, and the diamond fell out and the tooth grew back till there was no hole. Ever since, he been a minister. And my other grandfather, Gerald. I never knew him but he pure-blooded Cherokee so you know he was into some medicine.

"But listen, here's what happened. They make you study the Bible for weeks till you know everything by heart and the day of the baptism they dress you in a white robe. You waiting out in the hallway with all the other children shivering and biting your nails because you know you going to get dunked in the white light of the Lord. They call your name. Out I go. The choir is humming, *"Take me to the water / To be baptized."* The women is fanning and shouting 'Lord, Lord,' and they ask you, 'Do you know the names of the books of the Bible?' You shout out. 'GenesisExodusLeviticusNumbers, DeuteronomyJoshuaJudges-Ruth, FirstandSecondSamuels, FirstandSecondKings, FirstandSecondChronicles, EzraNehemiahEstherJob . . . ' And 'Do you take Jesus Christ,' they say, 'For your Savior and your Lord?' You say, 'I do.' 'Then on the confession of your faith, my brother, I baptize you in the name of the Father and the Son and the Holy Ghost' and they hold your head and down you go in your suit and your white robe. You come up gasping, grasping for air, sucking breath and thinking you going to drown, your eyes bugging out like a frog and then it's done. The choir comes up huge, *'LOOOORD,'* they singing, *'LOOORD.'* They give you a Bible with your name on it like it was engraved in heaven. You run down to your mama crying, then run back to the changing room where the next child is looking at you like you just come back from the dead and it's his turn to survive and you know you done been changed. You know you new life."

His words hung in the cold air. "No," I whispered. "We never had anything like that."

If The World Is Running Out

Let me still grow this fetus in my fat belly.
Let him be among the last to die.

In the spring when he's grown fully into his new body
I'll wrap him in a plaid pastel blanket the way
black women do in my neighborhood and cover
his dark face. We'll walk up along the freeway.
Papers are blown against the cyclone fence.
Lilacs high as trees explode next to the Evangelical Temple
across from the barbeque place.

On the bridge over the freeway, stop and look, child.
I want to show you this world. See how
we ride behind glass, hands clenched to wheels,
radio tuned to jazz to soothe
the cramped and hurried spine.

Here on the corner of 94 and Lexington three years back
is where your father was falsely arrested for aggravated robbery
because he looked like another black man in sunglasses.
Memory turns every pain to love. I still see
his hands on the Monte Carlo, legs spread,
gun at his temple, the angle of his wrists
in handcuffs as they pulled him to the car with the dogs
and he looked back, crying, "Call your father."

Your world, my son, slow St. Paul by the freeway.
At the corner, St. Peter Claver Catholic School
where black parents send their kids from Milton on down.
The rest go to Maxfield. You'll be bussed to Highland
with the Jews. Indians live up back behind the capitol.

Earth, 1981. Reagan inaugurated as president,
peanut butter $2.89 a pound, the 439th day of captivity
for the hostages in Iran. Your father at the factory
cutting huge rolls of tape. He comes home smelling
of adhesive and glue in his nappy hair.
Here is the SuperAmerica where men call out, "Say baby,
you in a fine and mellow mood today." I raise my thumb.

Here's discount liquors and the giant grocery store
with boxes stacked to ceiling of all the things

we trade our time for in this life: toilet paper,
celery, milk and bread. Walk you down aisles
to say I want you to love the sad world. Love your father's
hands on the congas Saturday night full moon.
Love your mother's rice and poems cooking in the kitchen.

Love the mongrel dog in the alley and the seven birdbaths
kept clean by that shriveled woman, the one with immaculate
    roses.
Love the smell of barbecue Memorial Day, ten in the morning,
Cadillacs washed and shining in front of the projects.
Love the chipped jelly jar your father drinks beer from.

Love the dust on it all thrown up by the freeway.
And the green dome of the cathedral spectral in orange light
at end of day. Love your father on his knees nightly
in the pale dark. Love your own dark skin in this world
you sleep. Take all you need of breath and night to feed you.

KATE GREEN

Journal: July 16, 1982

for James L. White (1936–1981)

In the last weeks, we didn't talk much.
That hot afternoon in the apartment
you made lemon chicken, I brought greens
from the garden and my newborn son. I was still tired
from the birth and my breasts hurt full of milk.
You made coffee, leaned back in your chair.
"It's sweet for you now, isn't it,"
you said and I said yes. You took your pills
in bright fluorescent colors, the utter blue
of the Elevil, the day grew hotter
and you were tired, too. I drove you to the bank.
The car was in direct sun, black parking lot
baking the baby and he fussed.
Monday you died of the bad heart
that broke you for years. I stood at your door
and rang and rang and the boy cried
in my arms, hungry for milk, hungry
for arms, you behind the door
in the late afternoon heat, waiting to be found.

The last good night we had, we sat in the bedroom
with the air conditioner on and you asked
to hold the baby. Then you read me from your journals
about dying while I rocked the boy to sleep.
There's no final sun or darkness enough
to know you're gone forever in the damp night.
July and the boats are still out on the water.
Curtains hang limp. Today is your funeral
down in Indianapolis at Christ Church
where angels and gladiolas walk your skin
to sleep in the earth but
you're off somewhere else in a humid heaven.

Sitting by a window with coffee is the earth
and your skin graying, the earth.
The blank paper before your last poem, earth,
and the saxophone old jazz on the radio, earth
down here on ground where you've left us.
Music was earth and poems and food.
Old bed with lumps, earth, and now the sky

seems blue and large above the survivors,
as if we knew this was finally only a place,
not the world at all, just a place
we bring our bodies to and leave them
on a late morning feeling tired
of the old heart and its crazy singing.

KATE GREEN

Don't Make Your Life Too Beautiful

Don't fix the three-foot hole in the plaster
over the stairway.
Don't sweep up the tiny specks of white
that gather in dust like stars.
Leave the hole under the fence
the dog dug in the marigolds
that never flowered.
You can look for hours at the pile
of shingles your neighbor ripped off his roof
and left to mold the green summer
with plenty of dark underneath for the beetles
and the worms to damp in.
Leave the rocks imbedded in odd places in the lawn.
And the black locust you cut down year after year—
you can let it become a tree after all,
towering thorns over the lilies and the peonies.
Look out the cracked window—
that broccoli just kept blooming
until the ice came down
and made us bend over our hands
in search of something we held and lost.
Leave it all exactly as it is.
There are heartaches enough to live for.
Leave the old worn boots stacked in the hall,
the rotten mattress in the flagstone basement.
Live out your ecstasy on earth
amid the flaking patio stones,
the boarded-up back door
and the rusty car.

MICHAEL DENNIS BROWNE has published these collections: *The Wife of Winter* (Scribner's, 1970), *Sun Exercises* (Red Studio Press, 1976), *The Sun Fetcher* (Carnegie-Mellon University Press, 1978), *Smoke from the Fires* (Carnegie-Mellon University Press, 1985). Browne has collaborated with the composer Stephen Paulus on several works, including song cycles, choral pieces, carols, songs for children and a one-act opera. Browne's awards include fellowships from the NEA and the Bush Foundation.

Browne has made his home in Minnesota since 1971. He is married to Lisa McLean and they have two children, Peter and Mary.

Fox

Driving fast down the country roads.
To a committee. A class.
When I stop for gas, a highway patrolman tells me
one of my lights is out.
Then he drives off to take up his position
behind a bush at the bottom of the hill
to wait for speeders.

Yesterday, a snake, black & green, coiled
down by the railroad tracks.
His mouth bloody, he moved slowly,
he looked like he was dying.
Boats being pulled up out of the water.
The dog ran into the lake
after the sticks the children threw,
and stood looking back at me from the gold water.

On TV, the faces of the captured Israeli pilots.
Syrian film of Israeli planes crashing,
martial music. The patrolman crouched behind the bush,
the mouth of the snake, hard & red,
his green-black body without ease,
a bent stick by him, as if maybe
a child had beaten him with it, maybe the same
child throwing sticks to the dog in the water.

Hurrying through Wisconsin.
Hundreds of black birds tossed up
from a cornfield, turning away. Arab or Israeli?
The man in the parked patrol car,
the sticks rushing, failing through the air.
County Road Q, Country Road E.
The committee meeting, waiting for me.

The fox! It is a fox! It is a red fox!
I slow up. He is in the road.
I slow. He moves into the grass, but not far.
He doesn't seem that afraid.
Look, look! I say to the white dog behind me.
Look, Snow Dog, a fox! He doesn't see him.
And this fox. What he does now is

MICHAEL DENNIS BROWNE

go a little further, & turn, & look at me.
I am braked, with the engine running, looking at him.

I say to him, Fox—you Israeli or Arab?
You are red; whose color is that?
Was it you brought blood
to the mouth of the snake? The patrolman
is waiting, the dog standing
in the gold water. Would you
run fetch, what would you
say to my students? He looks at me.

And I say, So go off, leave us, over
the edge of that hill, where we shan't see you.
Go on—as the white she-wolf can't,
who goes up & down, up & down
against her bars all day,
all night maybe.

Be fox for all of us, those in zoos,
in classrooms, those on committees,
neither Assistant Fox nor Associate Fox
but Full Fox, fox with tenure, runner
on any land, owner of nothing, anywhere,
fox beyond all farmers,
fox neither Israeli nor Arab,
fox the color of the fall & the hill.

And you, O fellow with my face,
do this for me; one day
come back to me, to my door,
show me my own crueller face, my face
as it really cruelly is, beyond what

a committee brings out in me, or the woman
I love when I have to leave her.
But no human hand, fox untouched, fox
among the apples & barns, O call out
in your own fox-voice through the air over Wisconsin
that is full of the falling
Arab & Israeli leaves, red, red,
locked together, falling, in spirals, burning . . .

be a realler, cleaner thing,
no snake with a broken body, no bent stick,
no patrolman crouched behind a bush
with bloody mouth, no stick thrown,
no beloved tamed dog in the water . . .

And let us pull up now out of the water
the boats, & call the leaves home
down out of the air, Arab or Israeli;
& you, my real red fox in Wisconsin,
as I let out the clutch & leave you,
you come back that time, be cruel then,
teach me your fox-stink even, more than now, as I
hurry, kind & fragrant, into committee,
& the leaves falling red, red.
And the fox runs on.

MICHAEL DENNIS BROWNE

Bach's Birthday

(Vernal Equinox, March 21, 1974)
for Mari

I

I am stuck in the First Invention.
The eleventh measure. I can't get it right,
co-ordinate the left hand and the right hand,
I play sharps for naturals, the left hand
is arthritic; it is awful.

Today is Bach's birthday.
Tonight I am taking a cherry pie
to my musical friend, who can play
Bach on organ and piano, both.
On the pie the bakery lady has squeezed
"Happy Birthday JSB" in white cream.
The lettering cost almost as much as the pie.

And I bet Mrs. Bach is busy,
baking pies for all those children
as she does every year on this day;
and tonight after supper
there will be a pie fight in paradise,
and the Bach kids will have at each other
hysterically, until they are spattered with
rhubarb, apple and cherry, pumpkin and mince,
peach and apricot, and custard of course,
and Mrs. Bach will be up half the night
running baths for—how many children was it?
(Twenty, at least!)

Today is windy, cold; but bright.
A thin snow on the streets.
You would not think our hemisphere
was leaning toward the sun again.
But it leans, all the records say so.
and my blood leans toward the sun too,
and toward Bach.

2

And here, as well as the Book of Inventions,
I have two other pages of Bach,
old, stained, torn
from my father's organ books,
too heavy to bring to America.
The first of the Eight Short Preludes and Fugues,
the one I would never tire of having him play;
I would sit in the sunlit church after mass,
the darkened church after Benediction,
and hear my father doing Bach's bidding
on the keyboards, fingering, fingering,
and doing the foot-dance with the pedals
and pushing in and pulling out stops,
busy Eddie, the musical man,
grandson of the Irish ferryman,
bringing us Bach, Bach.

The organ is called the King of Instruments.
Mari says she prefers it to the piano.
Last Sunday I heard her play it
for the first time — a time out of time —
those sounds that survive us.
Organ is like the French word "ouragan,"
meaning hurricane, and sometimes the organ
brings storms to my mind, where my father
is struggling in a small craft,
the seas tremendous.

3

Last night I fell asleep on the sofa
listening to the Matthew Passion.
Once I heard it in Helsinki,
In Holy Week, when I was twenty-one,
in a language I knew not one word of,
and felt I knew for that while
what the mystical men speak of,
that we are all one with another,
that we are each part of the other,
that all things are one.

MICHAEL DENNIS BROWNE

And this morning woke,
both animals on the floor by me
as if waiting for me to wake,
and the sky lightening already,
dawn beyond the branches,
day of Bach's birth, and the earth
leaning toward the sun as if
turning over from a great dark sleep,
and the sun beginning to climb
higher and higher daily, the North warming,
the lakes losing their ice.

I lean toward the sun
I lean toward the father.
I lean toward Bach on the hard keyboard.

Sometimes I think of myself
as a child, sometimes a giant,
and often it is the child who carries
the giant on his shoulders,
the giant weeping;
sometimes I am a young man made
of green wood, and there is
an arrow in my back, fired
by my father The Archer,
the last he loosed, and then lay back.

But now a man is climbing
the cliffs of Bach,
a man is swinging
from white rope to black rope
in the Bach gymnasium,
a man is sweating and shoveling pies
in the Bach bakery,
a man is watching over
millions of tiny clambering notes
in the Bach kindergarten,
garden of children,
Johann's millions of children buzzing
out of the Bach hives,
hot for the honey of the world.

4

And all of us trying to do
things we do not know how to,
now I am caught, now freed,
now I stop, now I begin again.
And Mari at the instrument, daughter of men,
building those sounds
in the limitless acres of the ear,
the oaks and harvests and hurrying skies of Bach,
as the North, whose children we are, leans
toward the sun, which is climbing, leans
toward Bach, who is climbing, the ice
streaming out of his hair,
and Death, Death, *wo bist du*, where, where is your sting?

MICHAEL DENNIS BROWNE

Talk To Me, Baby

1

A friend at a cocktail party tells me
of being on a fishing trip up North
and meeting some men from Illinois
who showed him how to clean and filet a fish properly;
and of how, when one particular pike
was stripped almost clean, almost all of him gone,
the jaw with the razory teeth opened
and some kind of cry came from the creature,
that head on the end of almost no body;
and the man with the knife said:
"Talk to me, baby."

2

Up in the Boundary Waters last weekend
I hooked a trout, my first, and played him.
I got him to the shallows
and tried to raise him. And the girls
got down into the water with my leather hat—
we hadn't brought a net—and I was yelling
"I've got a fish! I've got a fish!"
out into the evening, and the girls
tried to get him into the hat, and did once,
but then he was out again—a wriggle, a flap—
that fish jumped out of my hat!—
and the line, gone loose, jerked, snapped, and he was back
in the water, the hook in him.

And he didn't turn into
a glimmering girl, like he did for
young Willie Yeats,
nor was he a Jesus, like for Lawrence;
he just drifted head down near the shallows,
huge, the huge hook in him.
And Louis and Phil came up in the other
canoe, and we got the flashlight on him,
and tried to get hold of him. But then, somehow,
we lost him, drifting about, he was not there
but gone somewhere deeper into the water,
every minute darker; my hook in him.

MICHAEL DENNIS BROWNE   —61—

I hooked five or six snags after that, yelling
each time that each one was a fish, bigger
than the last. But I brought nothing living up.
And the other canoe went ghostly on the water,
and the pines were massed, dark, and stood and smelled
strong, like a bodyguard of dried fish.

   3

Breathing, my brother in my house,
and breathing, his wife beside him.

Breathing, my brother in America,
his body in my bed, her body.

Their tent the color of the sun in my garden.
And they are riding West.

And both of us riding West, brother,
since we swam out of the father,

heading, six years apart,
the same way.

The dog stares at me, not knowing
why I have not fed him.
The cat crying to come in.

Whom we feed, sustain us.
Who need us, we keep breathing for.

I have seen you, at supper with friends,
put your hands to the guitar strings

and bring strong music out, seen you
sit and pick out

a tune on the piano,
on a friend's penny whistle.

To hold an instrument, to play.
To hold a pen, to write.

To do as little harm as possible
in the universe, to help

all traveling people, West, West;
you are not traveling alone,

not ever; we all go with you;
only the body stays behind.

    4

When I stand on my island, a Napoleon,
one hand nailed to my chest, the writing hand;

when I can only *stare*
at the ocean, at the birds
running and turning against the light . . .

when I am
the Illinois man and his kind,
"Talk to me, baby,"

the one with the knife inside, sometimes,
the one you may meet on your travels,
the one behind you in the line to get on the bus,

the one arranging a deal in a phone booth
as you drive past,
when I become that thing I sometimes become,

I will go into
the green of this visit, the green
you asked me to try to see

after my earlier, darker poems for you —
and this, the fourth one, darker
than I meant, since the man with the knife

swam into it — O when that killer
stands over our city, our sleeping and loving places,
tent, canoe, cabin of sweet people —

I will hear with your ears
the songs of the birds of the new world
that so quicken you, and look for

their wings that flame and flash — there! there!
among the leaves and branches . . .

5

Too often I have wanted
to slip away, the hook in me,
to roll off the bed

and into the dark waters under it;
to drift, head down,
hide, hide, the hook in me;
to roll
in the wet ashes of the father,
wet with the death of the father,
and not try
to burn my way upward; the son, rising.
I swear to you now, I will survive,
rise up, and chant my way through these losses;

and you, you, brother, whatever that is,
same blood, you who swim
in the same waters,
you promise me to make *your* music too,
whatever the hurt;

O when we are almost only
mouth, when we are almost only a head
stuck on the pole of the body,
and the man says "Talk to me, baby,"
let's refuse him, brother, both, all of us,
and striking the spine like an instrument, inside,
like birds, with even the body broken,
our feathers fiery — there! there! — among
the leaves and branches, make
no sounds he will know;
like birds, my brother, birds of the new world, *sing*.

MICHAEL DENNIS BROWNE

RUTH ROSTON was born in Elgin, Illinois, and claims she was born again when, at age 53, she took poetry writing classes at the University of Minnesota. Her collection *I Live in the Watchmaker's Town*, was published by New Rivers Press in 1981. Her poems have appeared in journals and anthologies, including *25 Minnesota Poets #2* and *Anthology of Magazine Verse and Yearbook of American Poetry*, 1980. Poets & Writers, Inc. sponsored her reading in New York City in their 1984 Midwest Voices competition. Roston works for COMPAS in the Writers-and-Artists-in-the-Schools program and in the Dialogue Program.

Roston lives in St. Louis Park, Minnesota.

Symptoms

At 61 she keeps falling
in love — often twice
in one day: the Black
man who reads the
gas meter, the Zen Buddhist
who smiled, the Vietnamese
couple who bought the
delicatessen, the red-bearded
artist younger than
her son, an entire
woodwind quintet.

Her children drop their work,
rush home. This
is no fly-by-night change-
of-life symptom like the
poetry thing. This indiscriminate
falling in love reflects on
the whole family. They speak
in low voices as if attending
a sick bed, last rites.
                She
answers the door — she is
falling in love
with the candidate for the
44th district. He leaves her
his picture.

RUTH ROSTON

Sleight of Hand

> *. . . the Swedish Council-General in New York gives a*
> *dinner and reception for all Nobel laureates in the area. At the*
> *dinner . . . Isaac Bashevis Singer, who won the Nobel prize in*
> *Literature in 1978, happened to be talking to Robert W. Wilson*
> *and Arno A. Penzias who shared the 1978 Nobel Prize in*
> *Physics . . . for their joint discovery of cosmic black body*
> *radiation.*
>
> —Jeremy Bernstein, "Three Degrees
> Above Zero," *The New Yorker*
> August 20, 1984

And after dinner, shop talk
between magicians. Literature
sits down across from
Physics. *Vas machst du*, friends
among the stars? Mr. Singer
and the physicists swim backwards
until they bump creation
with their heads.

An antenna in
New Jersey picks up the hum
left over from the howl
the universe set up
on being born.
Dr. Penzias, Dr. Wilson—nothing
up their sleeves—pull photons
like prize rabbits from a hat.

Fossil photons these
that radiate three degrees above
zero Kelvin—
the mystic three—cooled down from
the billion of the first
three minutes into time. Which laureate
speaks pure Cabbalah?

After dinner, secrets of the trade
among magicians. Literature
asks if he can hear this remnant
of the hot big bang.
Sleight of hand from Dr. Wilson—

cassette for Mr. Singer.
On tape he hears a gentle hiss
"something like the sound of the sea."
What writer can resist the oldest
gossip in the universe?

Even a whisper, God knows, in the
right creator's ear can flower
into fables, cities, souls and
seasons new on earth. Literature
sits down across from Physics,
picks up a pen and writes in Yiddish:
Ein mul is gevein—
Once upon a time . . .

RUTH ROSTON

The Gingerbread Boy

Once upon a time a little old woman and a little old man . . .

Child of cinnamon, they cried,
child of cloves, molasses —
Glossy boy!

How old they seemed to their son
so newly deliciously sprung from the oven.
They were, in fact, in their early
twenties, joyful at what had risen
still warm from the pan to run
through the rooms of their lives.

Half-song, half-shout —
Run run as fast as you can —
He threw them a handful of
words as he ran.
Doors slammed behind him —
I am I am!
What strange wrong story has found them?

Asleep
he runs.
Screams there's a fox
in the closet. Asleep,
calls out to be saved
from a river
that laps at his bed.
See, nothing's there, they tell him —
only moonlight — shadows.

They're the first to say, looking back,
mistakes were made.

Still they remind each other
how the dough rolled out like a dream,
how they tailored the seamless
jacket — imported Swiss chocolate —
trimmed it with currant buttons.
Carefully, between them,
chose raisins for eyes — the eyes
of the Gingerbread Boy so finely

expressive no one resists them.
Then the mouth, that sweet
pink frosting—how girls
swarmed to touch it, licking their lips,
their fingers.

Mistakes were made.

They erased the cow, the horse, the barn.
Threshers and mowers—banished.
No pitchforks, no catcalls—Hey give us
a taste—c'mon, one bite!
Whole sound track wiped out.
Still in that hush, half-song
half-shout—*Run run as fast as you can*—
Still the rush of red fur in a dream,
the lap-slap of water.

They sketched in a city, a riddle
of rooms and streets.
Hired a new cast to stop him—
doctors lawyers judges priests—
who rose from neat desks,
case histories in hand,
to stream after the boy who ran
like the wind.   Child of cinnamon,
they cried, come be our good boy.
No!   Not now!   Not ever!
Words flew behind him.

Ahead, tall grass, the river.

The Gingerbread Boy stopped running.
Looked back.
All of them now—
what a long line they made—
stone still in their tracks—
arms raised, teeth
gleaming—farmhands, new
cast from the city wanting
only a taste, one bite.

RUTH ROSTON

Fox waits at the river's edge.
Dream Fox who lurked in the closet—
needed no key to get in—
or out. Half moonlight, half shadow.
Kindness itself, old Fox.
Jump on my tail—we'll swim
like a trout, like an eel—
cross the river in style.
Let them stand in that field forever.
Clever beguiling Fox.

What of the little old woman,
little old man, who were, in fact,
in their early twenties?
The end is not negotiable.
The water grows deeper.

From the tail, from the back,
from the sharp nose of Fox
the Gingerbread Boy looks behind him.
Those waiting on shore grow smaller.
He is back in his room at home.
He is breathless with running,
cries out to be saved from a river
that laps at his bed, rocks his bed
like a cradle.

Questionnaire

Have you found your own voice as a writer?
—Jerome Foundation

Voice—a slippery thing—betrays
mid-line, mid-poem.
Bar Mitzvah boy whose song
slides up an octave. We say it
kindly: his voice
is changing.

I saw a drowning once.
You know how sound's distorted
by the sea. Now water
enters all my lines.

Shall I sound like earth then,
echoing in caves, bat-squeak words
that hang there upside down—
high frequency that dogs
and dolphins hear?

I write to tell you
how it is with me in the cold
dark places of my mind.
I light this fire—
throw on all the words I know
to keep the beast outside.

I write the way I
learned to speak—I imitate,
go house to house with an empty
cup, borrow voices from a dozen
poets. And when I
steal outright, I leave a note—
unsigned.

RUTH ROSTON

JOHN ENGMAN was born in Minneapolis in 1949. His books include *Keeping Still, Mountain* (Galileo, 1984), and the limited edition volume, *Alcatraz* (Burning Deck Press, 1980). His poems appear frequently in such journals as *NER/BLQ, Iowa Review, Sonora Review, Antioch Review,* and have been anthologized in *Leaving the Bough: 50 Younger Poets of the 80s* (Internation Publishers) and *A Century in Two Decades* (Burning Deck Press). Engman's work has received several awards, including a Minnesota State Arts Board Fellowship.

Engman currently teaches at St. Olaf College in Northfield and as an Edelstein-Keller writer-in-residence at the University of Minnesota.

Atlantis

Everything that has been said for several centuries
is swept away by many hands and hurled through high windows
into a big hole my father calls *heaven* but I call *the sky*.
He looks angrily at me because I swore the human soul
was smaller and forlorn as any unmarked 8 oz. tin you pay
half-price for at the Railroad Salvage Grocery Store.

That was the night I thought he'd never learn
and I made foolish jokes about the boulevard in Minneapolis
where we both sat in darkness, watching yards where shadows
crawled between the bungalows like creatures from another
                                                            world
and all the mothers who would never learn had hung loads
of white shirts and nighties like ghosts who are waiting

for Christ to return. I was 21 years old.
Already I had said too much: an immigrant from Norway,
                                        Michigan,
my father often spoke about another Norway where the sun
rose once but never set. *This world couldn't be your first,*
he said, and by calling my ideas "wise" he shut me up. Age
21, my father thought what *his* father thought

was ridiculous, and railroaded here
to find another Michigan where he was sure silence had
the last word. Where he and his son could sit in darkness
swapping silences until between us we produced a third and final
silence big enough to house the wild inhabitants and keep alive
the kingdom of a sunken island we could swim to, should it rise.

JOHN ENGMAN

The Dolphins

In Florida, at the Aquatorium, dolphins
and my mother who had spoken with them in her native tongue,
Norwegian, nodded back and forth without understanding.
The man who made the dolphins jump with whips, blubber chunks
and smaller fish

sat on the deck with his logbook
balancing cost versus credit for the waterwalk and somersault
through flaming hoops. Father was off somewhere, admiring big ideas
glassy sea and miles and miles of white beach put into his head.
I was naked in Key West.

sunning in the buff,
eyeing girls as smooth as those I'd seen on travel posters.
Florida, my father said, was how he felt at first communion:
moonlit palms and bougainvillea coming on as holy spirits, bathers
in clogs and terrycloth, angels puffing up the hill to our motel.

"Everything is what they said it was,"
my mother said, on postcards. A dolphin on her postcards
flew from the Aquatorium into summer air as a trainer
bared his whipping arm, the way a novice floating too far down
is suddenly raised by his instructor, pulled by the hair.

We spent two weeks by the sea. Spent,
my father said, his whole payraise. We bought shells as souvenirs
and, it is impossible to say what we were thinking, saved
snapshots of the family escaping through a small Atlantic
painted on a huge screen. For 50¢ we could be anything:

Cuban dictators, divers, fishwives.
Pushing our heads through cutouts, posing as though in guillotines,
we became three dolphins who created monumental waves
on the mirrored sea. You can almost hear glass breaking.
Everything is what they said it was and we look free.

Keeping Still, Mountain

　　Looking through ads for drill-press
operators, caretakers, inventory analysts, beauticians
and warehouse helpers. I remembered what my father said
about Puritan ethics, and my heritage, the American Dream.
Although I've since forgotten what he said I know I spent
hours in a local cafeteria, paging through ads
and throwing I Ching.

　　Pennies clattered on the cold formica
as my hexagrams predicted full-time unemployment,
full-time meditation in the cafeteria: smoking cigarettes
and drinking coffee, firm and central in my own immense
fog area. The hexagrams knew all about my job hysteria,
and each hexagram contained some landscape with a missing
person, and a window with an ad for "help wanted."

　　I remember what my father said
when I told him I'd been advised against pursuing a career
by a book of ancient Chinese wisdom, he was silent.
Keeping still, mountain had advised me to remain detached
from real life, sitting in the local cafeteria and keeping
still, in meditation, smoking cigarettes and drinking coffee,
trying hard to understand the mountain.

　　It was my father who explained the mountain—
he brought me to a small plot in south Minneapolis, purchased
in the late thirties when real estate was cheap, my grave.
We stood in the mud by my grave. Uphill, near the mausoleum,
drill-press operators, caretakers, inventory analysts, beauticians
and warehouse helpers slumbered under granite and riderless
horses reared back from eternal torches sunk in yellow grass.
My grave was surrounded by white stones like a small crowd
of mourners whose faces had been worn off

　　by the long wait,
my father said, "If you dare knock the granite statues down
and pile these white stones high, dismantle the mausoleum
and unearth these rock-plaques, it could take you many long
　　　　　　　　　　　　　　　　　　　　　　　　　　　years
to work the whole earth bare, and still you'd never understand,
but if you did, the moment you finish, the mountain will be
　　there."

　　　　　　　　　　　　　　　　JOHN ENGMAN

Mushroom Clouds

During the final minutes of the raid
Miss Nurvak made us kneel with our heads buried
between our knees—the blast that ruined our lives
was her yardstick breaking in half and confetti
she shredded over us was fallout. One boy threw up
Cheerios beneath his desk and then ran from class
with wet pants. The rest of us survived the drill
for milk and cookies during Miss Nurvak's nightmare
sermon on the Red Menace.

Miss Nurvak,
who said we have nothing to fear but fear itself,
was scared half-to-death. The shelter beneath her garden
was stocked with canned goods and sterilized water,
rations against the coming days of radioactive ash.
In gas mask and green fatigues, Miss Nurvak
would needlepoint and listen to the gramophone
until the fatal firestorms passed and she raised
her periscope, searching for pupils
from the lost second-grade.

So life was more serious than I thought.
And it was Miss Nurvak who made me want to be a man
as hard and strong as the stone man on the stallion
in the park, the general with epaulets of pigeon shit.
I imagined myself in crash helmet and bulletproof vest,
Miss Nurvak's periscope rising from the blackened grass:
how happy she would be to see a successful graduate
of Central Elementary who had not been reduced to ash
and whose ideals had not been shaken by the atomic blast
and who pushed the culprit forward with his bayonet,
a boy with wet pants.

Poem With Sedative Effect

On the hospital unit where I work
a young girl wrote "I love you" on the walls

with excrement. A valentine of shit.
I wrote in the proper blank space, "Patient

has apparently expressed hard feelings
on the evening of the 25th." There are

no easy feelings in the books I've read
about the schizophrenic, psychopath,

psychotic. "There are feelings lodged between
my stomach and my mouth I can't cough up,"

she said. Then she wept because
the color of some old hallway linoleum

was very red. I knew
of no technical term for such an act, I wrote

"This patient does not seem to be herself."
I meant neither one of us knew who she was.

Pleased to be involved in the act of love
anyone could issue

the ugly, guttural noises she did.
She called every name of god

from Lucky Stars to Elohim.
Thorazine finally put her to sleep.

Because I am instructed to mistrust appearances
every fifteen minutes

I was an astronaut lost in space
and charted the position of the girl who never moved.

She was like a mural of the dark and stars.
In a blank space on the brainboard I wrote

"Patient has apparently slept last night."
And then I went home and wrote this poem at dawn.

JOHN ENGMAN

One Minute Of Night Sky

I worked for a year in the cellar
of an airtight clinic, trudged through a valley of cabinets
in a gray smock. My job was filing bulging folders of the dead:
I carried a wire basket through the alphabet, dumping envelopes
of aneurism, cancer and cerebral lesion into yawning racks.
I could travel decades in a few steps,

stop and page through a chart until
I was in the blue hills west of brain damage, dwindling hills
and rivers of red that met in flatlands on a black horizon,
ticker-tape from the electroencephalograph. Stapled on last
reports of death there was a small snapshot from the morgue,
a face no larger than my thumbprint.

The work made me sick.
Reading histories of tumors and fatal transplants
until the lines on graphs convulsed and snarled like wiring
come loose in a circuit for the mind of God. Once, I saw
close-ups of the malignancy which killed a man my age,
nothing much on the x-ray,

a blemish vague as memory,
a burr which swam through nervous systems into his brain.
I could have sworn he was staring back at me from his worn
snapshot but, of course, he wasn't. He couldn't. His eyes
were shut. I put him away with unusual force and heard
his chart jar the rack, as if something

small had gone off, a mousetrap.
The next day I quit. For the first night in weeks, I slept.
But in my deepest sleep, even now, if the chemicals balance
and tissues are ripe, a synapse forms the memory: iron
spring slips, the trap shuts, my eyes fly open and all
the darkness around me wakes.

Supposedly, each human being
has a built-in mechanism for one minute of knowing
he or she will someday die. One minute of night sky: life
going on across the street where someone greets darkness
with tins of food and drink, where someone listens, pauses
by the door and throws the bolt and lets the animal in.

Fame

Putting a page into the old Royal
gives me a weird sensation, not much else.
One room below they must imagine I'm writing
the great American poem, something very smart
that only I know, but this is my fame: dark ages
measured by mineral rings from my drinking glass,
several pages weighed down with ink, one ration
of light that falls on pyramids built by spiders,
beds you can pull from the wall.

What can I write?
"It was a dark and stormy night and I was howling
in the skyhigh streets—Juanita, where are you!
My love will never die or will die in five minutes
without you, we must work fast . . . " Oh my.
Once upon a time my life was easier between lines
where the mind stays blank, nothing to confess
but this: everything I know seldom fills a whole page.
"Someday, I'll be dead." That was my idea.
"Someday, I'll be dead, Juanita."
That was my poem.

And someday my critics will know
this simplemindedness, and all this aloneness,
was my fame: how I let everyone know how I feel
by weeping openly and showing off my weaknesses,
a few cents' worth of dust and lost ingredients
who wants to make a good impression, like a leaf,
in stone. So what if I stole my emotions: shyness
from the Murphy bed, ardor from the gooseneck lamp,
joy from the wooden chair? At least I let my poems
stay put until the last potluck, little sandwiches
Satan autographs with cheez-whiz. And someday,
Juanita, my fame will just be how useless
I am, beyond wanting and change. "Baby,
ain't no poems tonight,
just wind and rain."

JOHN ENGMAN

Another Word For Blue

On better days, I bathe with Wallace Stevens: dreaming his good
    dreams before I fall asleep, waves lapping, none of the poorly
    choreographed crashing they do around here, but waves
    that can read music.
And one afternoon, when I felt a new dream studying me
                                    closely,
    I kept my eyes shut and lay flat, but the dream flew off,
    leaving me alone again, asleep with reruns.
People who don't understand what it means to be an artist
    should be punished, and I know how: make them be one.
Make them write about their own mortal souls in the third
                                    person,
    make them enroll at college, where they will be forced to
                                    write
        creative things about a piece of driftwood, forced to write
    poems about their moods using colors like "cerulean,"
    another word for blue.
People don't understand that real artists are few and far between:
    bottles with messages in them wash up on the beach,
    always a heartbeat ahead of the sea.
It isn't always a matter of being in the right place at the right
    time, wearing clothing that makes them notice you: black
    satin jackets and green string ties, crocodile shoes.
Sometimes it's a matter of being in the wrong place at the wrong
    time, unsinkable as Ivory Soap, an aesthetic theory
    that isn't much more than a plain bad attitude.
All I ever wanted was an ice-cold beer and a booth with a view
    of the local scene, that, and the adulation of multitudes.
There's a little place about a block from here where they never
    heard of free verse.
When they say they took a bath, they don't mean they spent
    an hour soaking with Esthétique du Mal, they mean
    they lost big bucks at the track.
For all they care, Esthétique du Mal could be bathsalts.
They know two things: on planet earth "being yourself" doesn't
    mean much. And, there's no paycheck in pretending to be
    somebody else.
So when I give the waitress a look that says, oh yeh, I could
                                      have

been another Wallace Stevens — she gives me a look right back
  that says, oh yeh, so who needs two?
That's the kind of stuff that goes on in the poetry business.
And I am so pleased when I can refrain from expressing myself,
  refrain from saying anything new: I like saying the same
  old thing, words that stay put.
Words that don't go far, letting life remain a mystery for you.
Words I might say to a small group of friends someday, friends
  who will sponge me down whenever I begin raving about free
  verse back in the twentieth century, quoting at length
  from my own modest book of poems, a visionary work
  which sold poorly.

JOHN ENGMAN

DAVID MURA is a *sansei*, a third generation Japanese-American. His poetry has been published in many journals, *The American Poetry Review, The Kyoto Review*, and others. His essay "A Male Grief: Notes on Pornography and Addiction," won the Milkweed Creative Non-Fiction Award in 1985 and will be published as a chapbook by Milkweed Editions in 1987. Mura is currently writing poems, a book about living as a Japanese-American in Japan, and a novel about the relocation camps.

Mura writes: "I am concerned with alternative histories. . . . I want to question the ways we so often identify with the powerful, empathize with the victors, and, in so doing, let the complexity, energy, and pain of history slip from our grasp."

The Natives

Several months after we lost our way,
they began to appear, their quiet eyes
assuring us, their small painted legs
scurrying beside us. By then our radio
had been gutted by fungus, our captain's cheek
stunned by a single bullet; our ammo vanished
the first night we discovered our maps were useless,
our compasses a lie. (The sun and stars
seemed to wheel above us, each direction
north, each direction south.) The second week
forced us on snakes, monkeys, lizards, and toads;
we ate them raw over wet smoking fires.
Waking one morning we found a river boat
loaded with bodies hanging in the trees
like an ox on a sling, marking the stages
of flood. One of us thought he heard the whirr
of a chopper, but it was only the monsoon
drumming the leaves, soaking our skin so damp
you felt you could peel it back to scratch
the bones of your ankle. Gradually our names
fell from our mouths, never heard again.
Nights, faces glowing, we told stories of wolves,
and the jungle seemed colder, more a home.

And then we glimpsed them, like ghosts of children
darting through the trees, the curtain of rain;
we told each other nothing, hoping they'd vanish.
But one evening the leaves parted. Slowly
they emerged and took our hands, their striped
faces dripping, looking up in wonder
at our grizzled cheeks. Stumbling like gods
without powers, we carried on our backs
what they could not carry, the rusted grenades,
the ammoless rifles, barrels clotted with flies.
They waited years before they brought us
to their village, led us in circles till
time disappeared. Now, stone still, our feet
tangled with vines, we stand by their doorway
like soft-eyed virgins in the drilling rain;
the hair on our shoulders dangles and shines.

DAVID MURA

Huy Nguyen: Brothers, Drowning Cries

1

Shaking the snow from your hair, bowl cut
like an immigrant's, you hand me your assignment—
Compare and Contrast. Though your accent stumbles
like my grandfather's, you talk of Faulkner,
The Sound and the Fury. You mention Bergson,
whom you've read in French. *Duree.* How the moment lasts.
Your paper opens swimming the Mekong Delta.

2

As you lift your face, the sun flashes
down wrinkles of water; blue dragonflies
dart overhead. You hear your brother call.
You go under again, down, down, till you
reach the bottom, a fistful of river clay,
mold a ball in the dark, feel your lungs struggle,
waiting to burst—
                              Where is your brother?

Against the current's thick drag, stumble
to shore, the huts of fishermen—
My brother, my brother's drowned!

Faces emerge from dark doorways,
puzzled, trotting towards you, then
all of them running to the river,
diving and searching the bottom
not for clay but flesh,

and there the man

crawls up on the beach, your brother
slumped over his shoulder, bouncing up
and down as the man runs up and down,
water belching from your brother's mouth
but no air, no air; flings
your brother to the ground, bends,
puts mouth to your brother's lips,
blows in, blows out, until your brother's
chest expands once, once, and once,

and his eyes flutter open, not yet back
in this world, not yet recognizing the blue
of the sky, that your people see as happiness,
even happier than the sun.

3

It's five years since you sailed the South China Sea
and the night Thai pirates sliced your wife's finger for
a ring, then beat you senseless. You woke to a merchant ship
passing in silence, as if a mirage were shouting for help.
Later, in that camp in Manila, loudspeakers told the story
of a boat broken on an island reef, and the survivors
thrashing through the waves, giving up the ghost,
and the girl who reached the shore and watched
the others, one by one, fall from starvation,
as she drank after each rain from shells on the beach.
At last only her brother remained, his eyes staring
upwards at the wind and the sun, calling, calling her name. . . .
The camp went silent, then a baby, a woman sobbing.
And you knew someone was saved to tell the story.

4

Now, through Saigon, your mother hauls bowls of soup to sell
                                        at dawn,
Malaria numbs your brother's limbs: while he shivers on a cot in
                                        prison.
You write: "I wait for his death. Safe. Fat. World away." I red
                                        mark your English.
There was a jungle you fought in. There's a scar above your
                                        wrist.
A boy dives, splashes in the river and sinking, clutches his
                                        stomach, twists.
You're at the bus stop by Target. Snow is still falling, a fine
                                        blown mist.

DAVID MURA

The Hibakusha's *Letter (1955)*

(Hibakusha is a Japanese term for victims of the atomic bomb.)

The fields, Teruko-san, are threshed. A good
Harvest. All week I've seen farmers with torches
Bending to earth, releasing fires. The winds
Sweep ash across the roads, dirty my laundry
Hung on the fence. Prayer drums fill the streets,
And now the village starts to celebrate.
Last night Matsuo told me how he emptied
On a clump of rags beside the inn. Suddenly
The clump leaped up, groggy and cursing.
Matsuo finished, bowed, offered him a drink.
This morning I went out back to gossip
With my neighbor, an eighty-year old woman
Who prances like a mouse about her garden.
While she jabbered Matsuo cut her firewood;
Sweat poured from the scars he no longer marks.
Later I opened my shrine to its brass Buddha,
And fruit flies scattered from the bowl of plums
I've forgotten to change. Saved from the rubble
Burnt at the edges, my fiance's picture
Crumbled in my fingers. I lit him incense.
Matsuo says we can't drag each corpse behind us
Like a shadow. The eye blinks, a world's gone,
And the slow shudder at our shoulders says
We won't be back. This year I've changed my diet
And eat only rice, utskemono, tofu.
Sashimi sickens me, passion for raw meat.
Sister, remember how mother strangled chickens?
She twirled them in the air by their necks
Like a boy with a sling-shot. I'd watch in horror
Their bodies twitch, hung from her fist, and cry
That Buddha laid their karma in my stomach.
Like them we had no warning. Flames filled kimonos
With limbs of ash, and I wandered beneath
Smouldering *toriis* away from the city.
Of course you're right. We can't even play beauty
Or the taste of steel quickens our mouths.
I can't conceive, and though Matsuo says
It doesn't matter, my empty belly haunts me:

Why call myself a woman, him a man,
If on our island only ghosts can gather?
And yet, I can't deny it. There are times,
Teruko, I am happy. . . .
You say hibakushas should band together. Here
Fewer eyes cover us in shame. I wandered
Too far: My death flashed without, not within.
I can't come back. To beg the world's forgiveness
Gains so little, and monuments mean nothing.
I can't choose your way or even Matsuo's:
"Drink, Michiko, sake's the one surgeon
Doesn't cost or cut." Today, past fields black
And steaming, the pitch of night soil, I'll walk
Almost at peace. After a wind from hell,
The smell of burning now seems sweeter than flowers.

DAVID MURA

Song For Artaud, Fanon, Cesaire,
   Uncle Tom, Tonto and Mr. Moto

now I *kitsune*
open this song —

all the way from Shikoku and Shingu I axed the forest,
laid down spikes and pounded their heads, grabbed salmon
like arrows leaping from streams, all the way from Kotchi, from
                                                              Akao
and sir I want to complain of having to meet behind barbed
                                                              wires
too many ghost stricken people too many fools sir forgive me
I am the dance the drum the sneaky inscrutable body
and in each heel that stamps the dust a hundred bed lice
and a feast of fleas, mosquitoes and spiders come scurrying from
                                                              my toes
and the yellow fumes and flames that spume from my mouth
are only the spouting mystic metaphysics
of a Jap who knows at last my brothers
are creatures of adobe and Sand Creek and those who bowed
                                                              massa

yes, sir, all the good niggers and the mute buffalo herds
all the torrential unconsecrated nauseating flood,
each singing the old imperial clichés —
whip marks and sweat, harvest, bone and blood
yes, we shingles, the tuberculars, the descendents of plague
we live in the monstrous sarcophagi of your white cultivated
                                                              heart

and yes I am raving, incurable
and almost asphyxiated
and now proclaiming
I nail to my heart
and to the space between my balls
and here to the spongy dampness of my brain
something so emasculated it can only be
Witch rage and primal cohesion
an inveterate blackness

a torrential demonry
an infinite journey
from kissing ass

Isis and the Dragon, Voodoo and Hindu, Buddha and Shiva,
                              odors of Great Spirits
brothers, these are not hermetic, these are not easy lines
these are not thrown about without frightful black marks
or tossed in the manure of oxen as pork fat is given to the dogs
and here in my uterine mind something is cleaving, beating,
                              growling
and in a bath of vitriol it swims and sharpens its sleepy, delirious
                              teeth
and it is rising in Soweto, in Wounded Knee,

in Savannah and savannah, in the Indonesian junk shops
and the smell of the hanged man or the shoyu stained tables of
                              hanna
in the Andes and terrifying inner storms of the Caribbean
sordid, visionary alleys of São Paulo, the alchemical, Amazonian
                              jungles
and we are all good niggers, good gooks and japs, good spics
                              and rice eaters
saying mem sab, sahib, bawana, boss-san, señor, father,
                              heartthrob oh
honored and most unceasing, oh devisor and provider of our
                              own
obsequious, ubiquitous ugliness, which stares at you baboon-like,
                              banana-like
dwarf-like, tortoise-like, dirt-like, slant-eyed, kink-haired, ashen
                              and pansied
and brutally unredeemable, we are whirling about you, tartars of
                              the air
all the urinating, tarantula grasping, ant multiplying, succubused,
                              hothouse hordes
yes, it us, it us, we, we knockee, yes, sir, massa, boss-san, we
                              tearee down your door!

DAVID MURA

BARRIE JEAN BORICH was born in 1959 on the south side of Chicago. Her parents are schoolteachers, her family Slavic-Polish-Catholic-Chicagoans. Her work has been published recently in *Sing Heavenly Muse!* and *Milkweed Chronicle*. New poems are forthcoming in *Sinister Wisdom* and *The Greenfield Review*. Borich was part of the team that created the Minneapolis theater serial *TOKLAS MN, A Lesbian Soap Opera*. She also writes reviews for *Equal Time*, the Twin Cities lesbian and gay newspaper, and is one of the editors of *The Evergreen Chronicles*, a regional lesbian/gay literary journal.

Borich lives in South Minneapolis and makes a living as a free-lance writer and publicist.

Him, Her, The Other

1. HIM

I found my wife
with the woman next door in—
how should I say it?
a precarious position.
We were together just
the night before, sweating
like wrestlers, and when I came
she bit my neck.
All night she slept
with one warm thigh tossed
friendly over my waist.
I swear, we know each other
as well as my fingers know
their wrists.

With a woman it's not
like she's cheating—but what
does she want? They made friends
right away, got close like girls
do in high school, always whispering,
hands like paper fans
always covering their mouths.
She got the idea, she says
from a magazine. She doesn't
want to leave, she says,
but what's the way to touch her now,
like in that valley place
behind her waist that tastes
like salt.

Once she said it felt
like I was born
with my hands on her.
Now, when I work on Nautilus,
feel my muscles push hard as trucks
against the skin, my pores open
as faucets, I think how my body
will feel to her. Any man

BARRIE JEAN BORICH

could split open his fist
running into my chest.
She's never wanted a man
with muscles like puddles,
so why a woman? I don't remember
if she said her mother breastfed,
but my kids, sure as hell,
are gonna use that bottle.

I remember now,
once she said she liked motorbikes
cause the wind was hard enough,
but couldn't push her over
so her bones felt thick as trees.
But she's not that way,
cause I've been full up in her
and she's been around me tight
as the sleeve of a sweater.
I'd like to tear up her filthy
magazines, just so I could see
the pieces fall, but she's mean
when she's mad and I
don't want her to leave.

2. HER

I thought of it before the magazine,
and not just with her.
The picture wasn't something real,
the women's faces fuzzy like reflections
in a duck pond, and lacy underwear
looking like it itched something awful
but I couldn't move my eyes
from the page. It was familiar
like a face, someone
you see on the street
and you want to say hello
but you've never met.

We've been married long enough
that I could find him in a field

of naked men. I love the smell
of him sleeping, like skin just wet
from a run, when I burrow
into my usual hollow, breasts
pressed flat against his back.
With her—it's like a sound.
I can't place it,
but when it rings, the past
and present all roll together
and I don't know who or where I am,
I'm just happy.

Inside her body
I finally understand what the word
Communion means, and on Sundays
I think of her when I take
the wafer into my mouth
and it dissolves like burning
into my tongue. With him
we know each other but there's
a pane of glass between us.
We can see it all, but I can't
fall in.

I knew it was starting to end
when she started to want. Men need you
because most don't know how to care
for themselves, but women,
even just friends expect you
to sink fingers into their hearts
like it's pastry dough.
Still—I need her when myself
is piled all over my shoulders
like blocks stacked up
at a building site.

Now that he knows,
they're going to make
me choose. I've always worn
this clear jelly line
around the edges of my body,

BARRIE JEAN BORICH

a fence between myself
and the air that keeps
my soul from slipping away,
but lately it's changed
its shape. Nothing fits
the way it did before
and neither one of them
is enough.

3. THE OTHER

All my flesh
fell off my bones like dead meat
when he walked in
and I thought, he's going to kill
us, I know it. I felt like a kid
who just smashed her Dad's car
but he didn't lay a finger on us,
just stared, like someone asked a question
he was too dumb to answer.

I backed around the room clutching
sheets and clothes to my waist
and my fear smelled like a wet dog
but she just lay there,
squinting up, like there was TV
in the ceiling. I'd always
thought she kept running off
from me cause she was scared
he'd hurt us, but now
I know there's something else.

I don't think she loves him.
I think she loves me, but sometimes
it's such a long way to her eyes,
like she's watching from a tower.
Lately desperation rises in me
like nausea, and the meanness
tastes like metal in my mouth.
The closest we ever were
was the night she crawled from

his bed and in through my window.
I've got the instinct from living alone.
She's lucky I didn't knock her flat,
rattling the pane like a damn punk thief,
but she just laughed and peeled
off her robe. Later, holding her
and watching the night air fondle
the curtains I felt we were bound,
two sides of the same patterned cloth,
but it was weeks till the next time.

On days I didn't work
we used to start early,
yelling over the yard fence,
and I felt like a rope was reeling
me towards her. Then I'd come over,
or she'd come over, and we'd laugh
because it was afternoon and we
hadn't even cleaned up breakfast.
I was scared when she showed me
the magazine. I wanted to touch her,
that way, with my mouth,
but not that way.
I wanted something better,
my fingerprints on her skin,
my touch marking her,
permanent, like the scar
from vaccination that's pressed
into the flesh at the top of her long freckled arm.

Maybe if I'd asked first
she'd be staying with me now.
As it was, she just wrapped
her arms around my waist
and I couldn't lift my hands,
I couldn't lift my head,
like that game the kids play
where if you get touched
you're a statue.
Now my voice comes out yellow

BARRIE JEAN BORICH

and I can feel her squirm.
I ought to just tell her
stand with me, use both feet,
but I'm too scared
she could pull me off her
simple as she can slip
out of her clothes—
so I wait.

MICHAEL MOOS was born in 1949 and spent his childhood in the Red River Valley, on the edge of the plains. He is the author of *Hawk Hover* (Territorial Press, 1974), *Morning Windows* (New Rivers Press, 1983), and *A Long Way to See* (North Dakota Institute for Regional Studies, 1987). He has served as Associate Editor of *Dacotah Territory*, Assistant Editor of *Columbia: A Magazine of Poetry & Prose*, and Poetry Editor of *The Language of Light*, a Minnesota Writers-in-the-Schools anthology of children's writing. His work has received several awards, such as an NEA Fellowship and a Loft-McKnight Award for Poetry.

Moos is currently working on a fourth collection of poems and a novel. He lives in St. Paul.

The Archer

I draw the bow,
after leaving it for years,
unstrung, hanging on a wall.
I draw nock and feather
all the way back to the ear and hold . . .

And again it is the first time,
my father showing me how to stand,
feet apart, shoulders square,
heart turned away from the target.
He gives me an arrow,
and the pigskin grip dampens in my hand.
He tells me to forget the bull's eye
and, with both eyes open,
release. My fingers are weak;
the waxed string burns my arm,
and the shaft falls short.
The day fades,
and I grow some in my sleep.

When I wake he's gone.
So I spend the morning bending the limbs,
failing each time
to slip the loop over the tip.
Many times he returns with weeks of beard,
red stains on the knife.
Each fall I want to go,
but I'm too young.
So I learn to paint and fletch,
sharpen broadheads at night and wait.

And in time I'm ready to sit still
at the edge of a clearing at dusk,
where deer trails funnel through tall grass
into the open, into high wind.
I rise to my knees,
wanting the doe's blood.
I rehearse the story
but never connect.

MICHAEL MOOS

And one year
I stop dreaming of opening her lungs,
stop living to hoist the carcass
from a rafter with a rope.
I begin hunting something else,
not knowing I would come back,
when my father could no longer return,
to draw a man, a weapon, a life
into one weight.

. . . and after wanting so long
to give the arrow its freedom, I do.

Years Ahead

I'll see myself standing in line at Citibank,
thinking how a word is like a coin.
I'll remember these slashes of morning sky
pierced by steeples and steel wings,
these spring hours passing through me.
Again I'll board the 7th Avenue Express
with its generations of graffiti,
its gallery of curses and prayers.
I'll drop fifteen cents into the cup
of the blind saxophone player
as he staggers down the jammed aisle,
between the rows of exhausted faces,
who daily turn from each other's eyes,
glazed public eyes inching along
the gray columns of the *New York Times*,
their silent lips carving the underground air.
I'll click through the cold turnstile,
climb the rank stone steps,
feel the sun, an obsolete god,
draw winter out of my young bones.
Again I'll walk past the white statues
leaning out of Central park like ghosts.
I'll wonder about their names, their cracked eyes,
the men who cut them into life.
I'll hum an old blues tune,
and hope I live as long as Alberta Hunter.
I'll finally return to my own neighborhood
with its sweet stink of urine and rotting food,
its many languages and hidden pistols.
I'll sit at my favorite table
in the corner of the Hungarian Pastry Shop.
I'll watch the dusty ceiling fan turn.
I'll raise my glass of iced tea
with its quarter moon of lemon on the rim
to the green-eyed waitress and her earrings.
Again I'll love her distant stare.
I'll imagine Dante following Virgil
through these rubbled streets,
the cruel canyons of this burning island,
the scorched faces of these buildings

MICHAEL MOOS

blocking out the first star, the dark Atlantic
waiting for the lightbulbs to dim and die.
I won't care if these words transform nothing,
that these words only keep the record
seeing me through this one day,
that memory tricks me like a mirage as I age,
giving me back my life like a vapor.
I'll see my face in the glass of water before me.
I'll brush the fly away, sing the old renewal.
I'll remember myself remembering
how I walked with my father
across Amsterdam Avenue to Saint Johns,
its medieval granite bright an hour before dusk.
I'll keep writing until I see us
disappear behind the great bronze doors.
I'll close my eyes, and there in the dark
we'll stand together, alive,
lifting our eyes to the Lesser Rose,
the late light pouring through.

The Sparrows

If you could sit in my room,
at my table, look past my German ivy
and out my window that has no shade
you would fall in love with my sparrows
raising clouds in my gravel parking lot.
You would love their gray breasts.
You would love their common wings.
For ten minutes, before your day cluttered
with letters and bread and promises,
you would be filled and cleansed
with your own laughter. You would see
that no one and nothing needs you —
not the dusty hubcaps running with dew,
the girl passing on her yellow bicycle,
your past or the peach on the sill.
You would see them as priests
making war among stones.
You would want to join their ritual
as they peck the dry earth,
dance around the one crab apple
you imagine is their god. You would blink
and your blue eyes would become dark.
You would turn your feathered head on its side
and see two worlds at the same time.
You would thank the sky for distance
and the separation of beings.

MICHAEL MOOS

It Took Me A Moment To See

North on Minnesota 59,
hungry for the company of strangers,
I drive past the barren golf course,
the airport deserted at dusk,
the abandoned missile silos,
Oak Lake and Lower Badger Creek
to the Third Base Supper Club;
concrete deer grazing the dead lawn,
pink Styrofoam flamingoes
framing the Mediterranean door . . .

On the juke box Johnny Cash sings *I'm a Hero*,
then Jerry Lee Lewis rocks *Great Balls of Fire*.
Two migrant workers, a man and a woman,
get drunk on Gallo, forget their food,
their shack, the sound of their truck,
forget their children's voices,
the reason they crossed the border.
Wheat farmers in starched white shirts
break bread with their huge hands.
A late Easter lily blooms on the bar.

I raise my glass to the flame before me
and then to my dumb lips.
I think of the red vigil burning
in the dark at the side of the altar.
And it takes me only a moment to see
that it took me half my life,
driving all over this continent,
its cities crumbling at the mouths of rivers,
its small towns shrinking with the sun,
its highways crossing the haunted prairie,
its magic and glaciers and sextants
to see each moment is not perfect but *right*.

And driving home in the new dark,
between Thief River Falls and White Earth,
between winter and spring,

the presence of others
and the mirror in a nameless motel,
between the eye and the memory,
light years and the defeated heart
I see we are living and dying forever,
the night and the stars are not going away.

MICHAEL MOOS

LOUIS JENKINS was born and raised in Oklahoma. His poetry has been published in a number of magazines including *The American Poetry Review, Ironwood, Poetry East, The Paris Review,* and *Virginia Quarterly Review.* His poems have been included in these anthologies: *News of the Universe* (Sierra Club Books, 1980), *A Geography of Poets* (Bantam Books, 1979) and *Heartland II: Poets of the Midwest* (Northern Illinois University Press, 1975). He has published three chapbooks of his poetry. A larger collection of his prose poems, *An Almost Human Gesture,* will be published in 1987. His work was awarded a Bush Foundation Individual Artist Fellowship in 1979 and again in 1984.

Jenkins has lived in Duluth, Minnesota since 1971. He is married and is the father of a son.

Football

I take the snap from center, fake to the right, fade back . . .
I've got cover. I've got a receiver open downfield . . : What
the hell is this? This isn't a football it's a shoe, a man's brown
leather oxford. A cousin to a football maybe, the same skin, but
not the same. A thing made for the earth not the air. I realize
that this is a world where anything is possible and I understand,
also, that one often has to make do with what one has. I have
eaten pancakes, for instance, with that clear corn syrup on them
because there was no maple syrup and they weren't very good.
Well, anyway, this is different. (My man downfield is waving his
arms.) One has certain responsibilities, one has to make choices.
This isn't right and I'm not going to throw it.

LOUIS JENKINS

The Plagiarist

A fat teaching assistant has caught a freshman cheating on his exam and she stands now in the hallway displaying the evidence, telling the story to her colleagues: "I could tell by the way he looked. I could tell by his hands." With each detail the story expands, rooms are added, hallways, chandeliers, flights of stairs, and she sinks exhausted against a railing. More listeners arrive and she begins again. She seems thinner now, lighter. She rises, turns. She seems almost to be dancing. She clutches the paper of the wretched student. He holds her firmly, gently as they turn and turn across the marble floor. The lords and ladies fall back to watch as they move toward the balcony and the summer night. Below in the courtyard soldiers assemble, their brass and steel shining in the moonlight.

Violence On Television

It is best to turn on the set only after all the stations have gone off the air and just watch the snowfall. This is the other life you have been promising yourself; somewhere back in the woods, ten miles from the nearest town, and that just a wide place in the road with a tavern and a gas station. When you drive home, after midnight, half drunk, the roads are treacherous. And your wife is home alone, worried, looking anxiously out at the snow. This snow has been falling steadily for days, so steadily the snow plows can't keep up. So you drive slow, peering down the road. And there! Did you see it? Just at the edge of your headlight beams, something, a large animal, or a man, crossed the road. Stop. There he is among the birches, a tall man wearing a white suit. No, it isn't a man. Whatever it is it motions to you, an almost human gesture, then retreats farther into the woods. He stops and motions again. The snow is piling up all around the car. Are you coming?

LOUIS JENKINS

The Poet

He is young and thin with dark hair and a deep serious voice. He sips his coffee and says "I've found that it is a good idea to check the words you use in a dictionary. I keep a list. Here is the word *meadow*. Since I was a child the word *meadow* always had connotations of peace and beauty. Once I used *meadow* in a poem and as a matter of practice I looked the word up in a dictionary. I found that a *meadow* was a small piece of grassland used to graze animals . . . Somehow *meadow* was no longer a thing of beauty . . . " It is spring. A few cows are grazing in the muddy meadow. There are patches of blackened snow along the roadway. It is nearly dark and the ragged poplars at the end of the meadow have turned black. The animals, the stones, even the grass, everything near the earth darkens and above the *azure sky*.

Green Tomato

This morning
after the first frost,
there is a green tomato
among the kleenex
combs and loose change,
the more usual clutter
on the dresser.
That's the way it is
around here,
things picked up,
put down, lost
or forgotten.
Here is the possibility
of next year's crop,
even more,
in one green tomato.
It makes me smile
to see it there,
newly discovered
confident and
mysterious as the face
of my young son
who comes to the bedroom
early, ready to play.
There is no point in
my telling you too much
of what makes me
happy or sad.
I did not wake to find,
at this moment,
in this unlikely place,
only my own life.

LOUIS JENKINS

SUSAN MARIE SWANSON grew up in Illinois and Minnesota. Her poems have been published in *Primavera, The American Poetry Review, Milkweed Chronicle, HOW(ever)*, and other journals. Her work has received many awards: A Minnesota State Arts Board grant, the Loft-McKnight Award for Poetry, and periods in residence at the Ragdale Artist Colony. More recently, she studied Latin American-based Christian communities in an intensive seminar in Cuernavaca Mexico.

Since 1983, Swanson has worked in the COMPAS Writers-and-Artists-in-the-Schools program. She lives in St. Paul with her husband and their son, and enjoys spending time in Minnesota's rural communities and woods and parks.

Children In The Sun

This day, mine is one of the children in the sun,
a chariot that turns his hair white,
heats the pebbles and sand.
Andrés is waving his plastic sword.
Sarah points at her polka-dotted skirt.
Nabeel skids into his brother.
In a newer world, my little boy would be running on a planet
like a slice of bread or a painted plate,
but now we're nested on a globe of water, spun
around fusion's brilliant house.

The knotted three-year-olds repeat one after the other—
me neither, me neither, me neither.
That's a sand boy, a sand boy, yeah, a sand boy,
in a sand canoe.
Some of the kids are silent. Pablo, Adine, and Sabrina.
It is their time to live in an atmosphere
of warm air and grass. The three of them run in great
excitement, without destinations, a habit withdrawn
from the rest of us.

Each child is watched from an apartment window
which is at night a square light stuck close to the building.
Many people live here, in small rooms
with streaked tiles on the floors. Lately, I think
I would live here for the rest of my life.
But the children, the sun, and I are sometimes lonely
together, and angry at our life without chores or traditions.
Though they are tired of their kids and want to cook
and rest and make love,
I wish the parents would walk through
the doors, to their children in the sun.

Once, when the sun went down, I put on my gray sweater
and lay down under a tree. I want to know
what kind of tree. Children were hidden
in the hill where the sun fell down, full of sugar
from that sad lullaby with cake in it.
Near here is a swamp surrounded by a cyclone fence
that has lengths of barbed wire along the top.
God in heaven at night is strong, not beautiful.
It is hard to get to sleep.

SUSAN MARIE SWANSON

New Year's Morning

Were the Earth turned to blue paper and glass
under the long-fallen snow,
and below the bridge the barges
piloted by men made of fire,

how would we know?
Juncos flicker at the seeds
you hung in the ash tree. Creeks of cold
work their way into our rooms

while winter hours spin from the earth's hold.
Men and women are not windmills
spinning through the stars.
They are needing lotion and wheat

the winter long. When this leaf was green,
it was crumpled in my pocket
and now cannot be opened,
as if our little child could not stand up.

I have a calendar the size of your hand.
I used to want the old time back,
but the day we fell in love,
children fell into a crevice in Greece,

and women in Argentina wept
as soldiers cut hanks of their hair.
Beloved, I think God sends the time away
and away because, no matter what anyone tells,

the world is not small.

Thanksgiving

1 CALENDARS

The crab apple trees, having lost most of their leaves,
are all little apples and light. As geese call out—
Prepare! Prepare!—and begin angled flight,

we ready ourselves for thankfulness.
Walking here this morning, I know almost nothing.
It could be that the century has moved on without me,
or duty will knock and find me holding
the wrong tools. We have only body and mind.
There are potatoes to peel, and part of the planet
burns to make our ovens hot.

In the village of my heart, one man is swinging a scythe
while his daughter runs across the field to catch
a goat. Their calendar is heavens

and plants. I think of the village
when I swim laps at the pool.
One is skipping stones on a northern ocean.
One has a fever. One warms her hands
by the coffeepot at the church.

Were I a water bird, I would care for the water,
not knowing even the color of my feathers.
I would be aware of the end of the world and understand
the look of my niche from a great height.

The swimming pool is marked with long lines to follow.
At one end, they plunge deeper into the ground, but I stay
on the surface with the others. We are wearing slick caps,
and—why is it?—we are trying very hard. Oh how I wish
the friend I have lost was at the pool with me!

2 HARVEST

People who belong together are straggling apart
through fields and city, pulling at their collars
and tugging loose buttons off their coats.
November put tears in their eyes.

SUSAN MARIE SWANSON

They don't carry compasses. I want to build a bonfire,
right here, for them to walk to. They could speak.
They would know a little about healing
and the devil. They might plant a forest
to replace the wood that is burning. Some have tassels,
fringes—caught up in the wind

over a hillside of grain and straw. Hands
bend cut straw into reindeer and geese,
hands spin it into gold. The grain journeys
through the mill for cereal and bread . . .
A small and dear harvest it is, the harvest of the mind.

I do not know how evil began,
but I believe it is made of three elements:
plutonium, hail, and will on fire.
Tiny children are falling to ground and floors everywhere,
wanting to walk. Sicknesses cackle into their bodies.
We work to vaccinate them.

Do we need more power than that?
It's all we can do to sweep until a single
lost coin is retrieved. Still we press hard away from
our families or from the desire to be whole,
to be plain.
What do you need to tell your love before you die?

Paul said to the Philippians:
I thank my God in all my remembrance of you.
We are writing letters with our lives. A letter is made
and carried out of time on paper easily torn.
A letter is small.
It makes use of a language larger than the sun.

3 CRANBERRIES

Once, two girls were washing white berries at the creek.
When a trout glimmered to the surface,
they scattered berries onto the water.
For the raccoons who capered to the edge of the creek,
they tossed berries onto the rocks.

They threw berries into the grass for deer and mice.
Night fell.
The girls carried the rest of the sweet berries home.
As they reached the threshold,
the loons of the lake and the wolves of the wood
began their penetrating cries.
The berries, slung deep in baskets,
turned a bitter and deep red.

Today we have candles, tomorrow we will be poor.
When the uninvited guest arrives, gray-skinned
and smelling of urine, to take her place at table,
what do we say to her? Then, what will we give up?
She was reaching awkwardly for my baby
on the city bus. We all will collapse one day,

like water pumped away from the earth and released, heavy
and beautiful. At night when I come from the bright hallway,
the baby's bed is black. I have to stand there

until what I know appears. This November,
I am thankful for getting used to the dark,
for the planet, turning. The cranberries have been cooked
with oranges and honey, while the year slips away
on a sled of light and sleet. I am thankful
for the city that cannot be understood,
for the tree where the world began, for the angels
and strangers climbing up and down.

SUSAN MARIE SWANSON

DANIEL BACHHUBER was born in Milwaukee, Wisconsin in 1951. His work has been published in *Milkweed Chronicle, The Christian Science Monitor, The Iowa Review* and *The Sackbut Review*. His time studying contemporary poetry as a graduate student at the University of Iowa led him to write poetry, although it was not until 1981 that he began to write in earnest, the year he completed an M.F.A. at the University of Wisconsin–Milwaukee.

Bachhuber moved to Minnesota in 1981. He later spent a year in Italy to become licensed to teach Montessori elementary school, his current profession. He and his wife, Margaret Todd Maitland, have a young son and live in St. Paul.

Bird

Once you have wings,
The whole world turns upside down.
You glide and soar away—
The world backs up
And watches you,
Like a giant eye
Hanging surprised for an instant, in orbit.
And all that happened
Was what wanted to happen.
The air feels cold on your face and body
And then warm and then wonderful
As the slim, courageous beak,
The precise eyes,
The splendid feathers
find their place.
You used to be a dinosaur:
Always surprised by the coldness of the cold,
The iciness of ice,
The gloss on glaciers as they moved closer.
But some loving spirit hollowed out your bones
While you slept;
It took the spine out of your tail
Where it didn't belong anyway
And added quill feathers,
Lots of them.
It put air sacs in your belly to lighten the weight,
And the tough muscles
Of those terrible forepaws
It transformed into useful wings
That rose and fell with the motion of waves
Scintillating with a flurry of feathers.
And, last but not least,
It knocked all your teeth out one by one
And added a beak:
This last act,
Mean though it may have seemed,
Was just to remind you
The climb wasn't easy.

DANIEL BACHHUBER

Snowstorm

In mid-July we gave birth prematurely.
Skinless, purple,
our bruised fruit rested in my palm,
each joint and limb perfect,
the fingernails like minute shells,
the half-moons of her peaceful eyelids.

I remember one detail
more sharply than the others:
her wrists crossed tightly on her chest
like an explorer dead in a snowstorm
paralyzed by the coldness of a new world.

The nurses helped us.
We followed the proper rituals of naming and burial.
We built a scrapbook of the letters from friends,
the tiny feet imprinted in black on the first page.
No photograph, we decided—
it would violate the subtle presence
that watches our lives
and grieves for us.

Playing Second Base

There was that perfect practice.
No matter what Pat Bolger hammered to the infield
We caught it: Daley at third,
Larkin at short and me playing second base,
Almost crying for the sake of something gone right.
Caught in the rhythm
Of crack and plunk and whoosh,
I felt wings growing on my back—
The scent of angels.
                    A hard
Grounder right at me one of those
Skidders that backs up while it shoots forward
And I was on the thing as it poured
Into my glove like wine into a loving cup,
Not a drop spilled,
But my legs rose off the ground,
My knees bent and arranged a little kick
Before I flung it to first.
A kind of tittering chortle passed from Larkin's lips,
Rounded the basepaths quicker than a ball
Stung glove to glove around the horn
And nailed my heart to a tree.

DANIEL BACHHUBER

That Single Candle

His Dad said, "Put out the candle
When you come to bed,"
But Mike left it burning on the windowsill.

I remember when the house burned down:
The whole family stood in nightgowns
And robes two days before Christmas,
All of them crying, even the father,
So frightened in the cold wind and snow
Until the neighbors came and the gone house
Prickled the chill air with needles of light.

Later, in high school,
Mike would rifle his parent's liquor cabinet,
Grab the dry vermouth by the neck,
Guzzle down half a pint in eight seconds.
Or we'd coast his Mom's banana-yellow Bonneville
Silently down the long driveway:
Out of earshot, we'd fire it up,
Streak at three a.m. through the hushed boulevards.
He scared me to death,
Aiming our lives at parked cars,
Veering away at the last instant
With uncanny accuracy.
Once he walked a narrow ledge,
A sheer three-story drop on one side,
And held us breathless,
That condition of being suspended outside of time
Which is sometimes experienced at the circus.

I wonder now if he blamed himself for carelessness,
Or for the truth of his own life—
That single candle.
I wonder if the fire still burned in him,
The ghastly shadows of his family
Flickering on the white lawn,
A desperate ten-year-old
For whom experience overfilled
The modest container of his heart.

Unable To Sleep

I turned off my transistor radio at nine,
I had to be asleep by nine-fifteen
Because at five a.m. my paper route had to happen
And it would be cold on the street.

I loved the smell of newsprint Saturday mornings,
Loved the ripe jelly rolls
At the just opening bakery.
But weekdays were different.

I was afraid of Mrs. Connally:
Heavy, freckled, balding,
She punished us with three hours of homework,
Each night pressuring my scheduled sleep.

My ears coiled around the sound of the clock,
A big brass model I bought
With first money on the route.
My eyes kept springing open.

I forced myself deeper into the groove of my bed,
Shut my eyes and sealed them with my fists.
The refrigerator chugged on downstairs,
The furnace ticked and huffed hot air up the chute.

The voice of Mary Wells sang in my brain,
"There's nothing you can do cuz I'm stuck like glue
To my guy, my guy . . . ":
The few words I could remember

Echoing and re-echoing,
Positioning themselves like a stick in the window,
Through which spilled
The blackness of the world.

DANIEL BACHHUBER

Patricia Kirkpatrick grew up in Des Moines, Iowa. A letterpress chapbook of her poems, *Learning to Read*, was published by Meadow Press in 1982. Her poetry has appeared in *Ironwood, HOW(ever), Milkweed Chronicle*, and *25 Minnesota Poets*. Kirkpatrick received the 1983 Montalvo Poetry Award, and she was selected for The Loft's WRITERS ON STAGE theater project in 1984. She has worked as a writer, teacher, and consultant for a number of nationally recognized writing projects and currently teaches at Hamline University.

After living for ten years in San Francisco, in 1983 Kirkpatrick and her husband, playwright Bart Schneider, moved to the midwest, to St. Paul, where they recently celebrated the birth of their daughter.

Circle

I pictured the world before it was made,
a ball in darkness. Darkness.
I had to keep starting over.

I pictured a ring, a circle
from a burnt-down fire.
I pictured it glowing but mostly I picture it grey
with ashes.
I pictured flowers. Purple violets.

Dawn had pitched its pale stake.

I saw the child born. I pictured
a circle without a person.
The fur of the wet head glistened,
a crown shining
while the room was silent with
something determined
to come into it with us.

We looked out the window to trees and said "oak"
should be one of the names
The time went from waiting
to the child the man pulled from the woman
and laid on her stomach.
Someone handed me scissors,
said to cut,
so I cut the throbbing cord.

The child was given to the world and washed.

The woman got up, left a mark on the sheet
where she squatted,
a white footprint in the red circle of blood.

PATRICIA KIRKPATRICK

Hidden

Apples too green to eat I still would pocket.
Grandmother shakes her finger but I flee.
Run down to the grocer of grapefruit and sawdust
too old to see my hands in the penny box of licorice.
I learn what I'm not given I can take.
My name falls from branches while I stand in the alley to eat.
Closer to ground locusts blister the tree with their skins.
Mother pushes clothes through the turns of a wringer routinely.
An owl bores the blind afternoon with his hooting.
I take my nap naked and wake to hands touching me.

We move to the new house and father plows the garden under.
Father says 'your mother' pours the night its shot of whiskey Mother fixes
dinner we do what we're told but Mother still gets
pneumonia lies upside down with a bowl to let the stuff in her lungs into.
The thud of what doesn't belong always belongs to us.
After dinner, homework, Father's good at the focus of each word
    on a line of its own.
I write *my mother put a tortoise shell comb in her hair to wear as*
    adornment.
Things that happen are hidden, I am always trying to find them.
My sisters know where the female rabbit suckles wet young in
    the grass.
Father, if you could love something you could love all of us.

White snow and the houses heap their cold into shadows.
The man with coal comes to deliver his load of blackness
and we will always be the children who watched it go down.
The baby swallows money and has to be shaken.
We can't sleep so Mother walks the lumber of cows to our beds.
I replace stealing with dreaming.
A man arrives with a suitcase, says I can come if no one comes
    with me.
The cover I wake under is a mountain my fingertips wander.
Each song has a little rise over which the music must pass
and the only word left is forgiveness.

First Lullabye

Someone knows the sex of our child.
"Don't tell us," we said.
The child swims in the sea of the womb.
Let her be a boy now if this is his time.

Let him sleep on the crescent moon
of her spine in the dark without learning
the ways of this world too soon.
Let the spring tulips open, red or yellow

no matter to the trembling
waterdrop beating inside her.
Let the world's first word for our child
be the world's secret a little longer.

PATRICIA KIRKPATRICK

Water In The Tropics
Or The Woman Who Fell In The River

I read in a book about a rain that falls from the mist after sunset. Water in the tropics like the soft feathers under a wing. Serein. Sometimes the fog is like that, blurred mist, and the doves sit right on the fire escape. Their sound is inside them, a pit of song like the core of an apricot holding soft flesh to the seed.

And they put a white hen on the little girl's head where it started to scratch up her scalp, then quit, which meant she was still a virgin. *For the sound of her body was clear.* She was the one who sat in the river. At night the hunters of men came to her village. She was thrown in the holds, raped by white sailors, and on the island gave birth to a daughter whose mistress, Xaviere, called her "Two-Souls" for the different color of each of her eyes. Those were slave islands. *They worked like oxen, and when their work was done, they stood still, like oxen.* Two-Souls remembered her mother: she was one of the ones with her face incised, who still talked the animal language and was called "Wilding."

The fog is for most of the morning unless you get out of the city. Old streets where the bricks hum when you drive over them are called "singing." We drove over at dusk. Judy showed us where the dog was chained to a car, the car itself gutted, its tires spread like soft fat in the dirt. Judy lives beside that family with rats in the yard: old tubs, Frigidaires, broken televisions. There's a girl in the house. Her back is ribboned, flesh stands up, shiny and mauve against her black skin. At night her brothers talk about shooting and if their little bitch sister ever talks to that white woman next door again they'll beat the shit out of her. She lies wide awake in her bed; she's got to stay hidden until she can't hear them anymore. Already she's bled a little but her breasts don't show through a sweater yet and each day her hair is braided and she walks to school with a friend.

It will come off, the fog over water, as white threads can be scooped out of melon.
   These years are obscure and their chronicle uncertain.
Now the girl never speaks to her and Judy tries not to think about it.

Still, a girl gets an idea and goes in, the silt itself solid some places, like cool bars of soap although she imagines unscaled fish and floats, her feet don't touch bottom. She feels the little fish too, their quick mouths like petals opening all over her. There is something new started. Maybe she doesn't say anything, but while everyone sleeps she is learning the blue-lap of the wave rising right up on the sand. The sound of her body is clear.

PATRICIA KIRKPATRICK

Against A Winter Sky

These trees, their sutures stitched
like fragile black calligraphies
against a winter sky.
Inside the radiators clack
and tease.

The house appears to be
an open boat
the oaks can enter, bare
until the snow comes.
I set myself afloat

against a season I must get
through.
I write from cold, cold comes
and temperature is pitched
with memory, which has a season too.

Sometimes she comes, the girl
I was and what I needed when she craved
the mirror at the bottom of the stairs,
the last step where she sat.

The face she questioned, posed,
the question she faced when
I questioned what things meant.
Winter was always a season that kept
me home, now the same as then.

My eyes are grey, my eyes
are grey I said.
Father's the one who tells me no.
Mother's the beautiful loser.
Desire is the prayer I mouth in my dark bed.

No one breaks me into daughter now
except the sky. Despair
makes me remember. Nothing eases this
despair except desire, the wish for something, holds
the swollen tips of branches against the freezing air.

Ashland At Arundel
for Bart

The evening holds the water
against the dusk,
the mower against the growth,
the child against all the rest
of her life that could not touch

white chairs and cups in which the tea
is hot and sweetens after dinner.
I hold this corner of the porch
and repeat the notions signs taught me: *stop*,

okay and *go*. A blue car leaves
a boy off: he was born with the right to expect
supper and socks
and down the street a boy like that
was beaten to death in the snow.

Fences for stopping, street lights for going on.
We endure because we learn
less than what we want to know.
Grandmother held us each
in her lap and counted out pennies and mints
yet she couldn't keep her son
from his father's hand.
His story went on with a gun and blood
she lives to finger the memory of.
Bravely she sits in her chair at the home,
her life in a drawer beside the bed.

I don't say home to mean the frame
and tiny cross-stitch she loved
but where they make you what their notion is.

Tonight I join the others who park
their cars in front of lawns and linger
a bit on sidewalks,
then come in
to lilacs, those clusters of sweet
pale crowns, the ones we pick
and those we only picture—the claims
of memory and imagination are equal.

PATRICIA KIRKPATRICK

Pain is not a thing that falls
away. Someone recalled
a photograph of the broken
lilac branch, its light
flowing like a blow torch.

I take both the meaning and the song
to be the truth
and what the truth won't go without.

We are given to our lives.
Our offering is steady, we come
with blossoming and rot.

I wake saying now
is the time I want to make
my life a home.

JOHN CALVIN REZMERSKI was born in Pennsylvania in 1942 and moved to Minnesota in 1967, about the time he began to publish poetry. His books are *Held for Questioning* (University of Missouri Press, 1969), *An American Gallery* (Three Rivers Press, 1977), *The Dreams of Bela Lugosi* (Knife River Press, 1977), and *Growing Down* (Minnesota Writers' Publishing House/Westerheim Press, 1982). Rezmerski helped launch both the Minnesota Writers' Publishing House and Minnesota Poetry Outloud. Since 1980, he has continued to write poetry but has worked more at editing other people's books—poetry, fiction and nonfiction—and at free-lance journalism and editing.

Rezmerski is living in England in 1987.

A Long Dream

All the people who will ever live anywhere are in one long room. I stand by the door while they file out on their way to the world. Some children first, I kiss each one, tell them I love them. They are all beautiful and the women and men who all follow are youthful and smiling and slim. I never get tired kissing billions of them and when I say I love them I am telling the truth.

Then an old man comes out. He is twisted and filthy. Putrid. His face all scarred. A running sore on his upper lip. His right eye oozing. He moves toward me in spasms. I hesitate. I hesitate.

I shut my eyes tight and kiss him on the lips, like a little boy kissing my father again in spite of his breath of stale tobacco. I put my hands on his arms. I love you, I say, and open my eyes.

It is my father, young as he was when I was three, as though he had been disguised to test me. People keep coming, single file, now to kiss him, not me. He refuses no one, not even those who stink or have no faces left, and I stay by his side admiring him. By the time he is done, he is old, and broken down, with a running sore on his lip.

JOHN CALVIN REZMERSKI

Growing Down

If you are ten years old
I am too late to tell you
what I would have told
all you nine-year olds:
that at eight years old
you would have been better off
if you were still seven,
but not as well off
as if you were still six,
which is when things
start to go bad:
because you are not
five anymore and
have forgotten everything
you knew at four.
So you three-year olds
are the ones I really
want to talk to,
because you remember
what it was like
to be two and a half
when people were just
beginning to talk to you
for fun, but
not baby talk like
when you were two
and they treated you
like one-year olds.
Anybody knows better
than to talk to a one-year old.
They don't listen.

Why Henry Thoreau
Never Married

Something about a woman
is green and secret
like a pod of beans.
So I began by studying
beans,
folding back the shells
looking for seeds,
splitting open each seed
looking for the soul of the bean,
looking for some reason to say
women are holy.
I thought to start
I could pick them over,
plant them, harvest them,
go out in the field and sit with them,
cut away the clutching weeds around them,
handle them, finger them,
take them to my house,
talk to them,
taste them, sort out
the sweet and the starchy.
I could give each one a separate name,
I could know all their secrets.
Cell by cell,
I could know them all.

JOHN CALVIN REZMERSKI

The Time Being

(after Paul Granlund's sculpture)

A man coming forward
leaves a hole in time
he cannot see any more
than the hole in space
where he just was.
He can pivot, flex,
bend, reach, spin,
chase himself in circles,
and never see it.
He leaves it all behind,
the print of the face,
the work of the hands,
the mark of the nerves,
like a trail of coins
dropped for someone else
to collect or spend.
He peels the past forward,
rips the future back.
He is a wedge in time.
He moves at angles
to everything,
splits time
into the geometry of dance.
His sweat
has the smell of forever.
Too much energy
to stay quiet
on any surface,
he reaches up, and out,
to eat the stars.
For him
the sun is gold,
the moon is silver,
the earth
is round
and worth saving.

After The Attack

When they crawled out of the cellars
of the burned houses,
and came dirty and dripping
out of the sloughs
and saw how many of the dead were their children
and how bright the children's blood was
next to the dull adult blood,
and when they saw
how quickly flies light
and maggots are born
and saw
how hard it is to tell
human guts from a split hog's
and when they understood
how hated they were
they swallowed their tears
and puked
and saw the puke and tears
on the grass with the blood
and puked again.
And they wailed hoarse prayers
to let it not be real,
not be real children,
let them belong to somebody else,
let them be lambs,
let them be beasts,
let them be alive again,
let me not know them by name.
No prayer is big enough for some things.

JOHN CALVIN REZMERSKI

For Martin Luther King, Jr.

After all the formal baptisms of water,
without ceremony
he entered the Jordan of his own blood.

We have been looking for gurus
to move quietly among us
and have not heard the thunder
of souls breaking out of bodies.

Life and death are on television,
dancing
in the words of followers and leaders,
electric and indistinct.
CBS and NBC cannot weep. In their pictures
even tears seem black and white.
No blood drips from the screen
onto my living room floor. Yet,
I walk around it. Lord,
I say to someone I have never seen,
Make me transparent.
Make us all transparent.

ROSEANN LLOYD was born in Missouri and moved to Minnesota when she was fourteen. Her first book, *Tap Dancing for Big Mom*, was published by New Rivers Press, in 1986. Her poems have appeared in *Sinister Wisdom, Contact/II, The Greenfield Review, 13th Moon*, and other journals. Her meditations are included in *Today's Gift* (Hazelden, 1985). Lloyd's current project is co-translating the Norwegian novel, *The House with the Blind, Glass Windows*, by Herbjørg Wassmo, to be published by Seal Press in the fall of 1987.

Lloyd writes: "I send my list for The Best of '87: walking outside all winter, *Graceland*, silvery raccoons in the middle of the city, the zen of spackling, reading Alice Miller, my daughter's energy, writing list poems."

Words Before They Gather

Sometimes making love
it settles in my left thigh
that place the stairs hit
the time the drunk landlord left the trapdoor up
and lights off. My brother
fell down that cellar once, too, but that fall
wasn't what killed him. As for the landlord,
he is not dead, he's outliving his sister Marie
who bailed him out thirty years
and went real fast. There's no accounting for it.

Cigarette butts in the tub, I yell
at my brother, *Who do you think you are?*
It comes on, his voice,
You've got a raunchy mouth, woman,
as if we're taking arguments
to old age together, until I remember
him dead at twenty, not even half
a life. Our father moaned, *This death
is selfish.* I hear my voice answering,
Only the dead can know. Left behind
at the funeral, we can't know, we try, how
to manage living. How helpless all of us
were that day: the friend who stood by me
wearing her dead mother's coat of unborn lamb—
my mother, the child just buried
the one she loves best of all—the lover
who spooned chilled yogurt in my mouth, afraid
to father children—the man who was my husband
accusing, *The trouble
with you is your family,
drunk, divorced or dead.*

There's no accounting for it, though
there's reason enough. This anger
at the havoc they leave behind.
But, again, the dead, selfish? Only they
can know. One thing we can know
that's good and selfish
is making love

ROSEANN LLOYD

even when it brings them back—sprawled
there, half-conscious
on the moist and graying sheets.

These voices
for the graves of the living.
When I shoot off my mouth, I know I'm alive.

Southeast Asia, Second Grade

When the art class washes black
over their secret crayola drawings
Blong's Spiderman
pulls a green net across
the watery page. When we write
poems that begin *I Remember*
Blong designs
a Mercedes limousine, the military
detail, exact. In dream
poems, he colors a ship
with two anchors
a ship whose stars and stripes
shine turquoise, orange, and green.
He prints slowly
I'm the one who eats ghosts.
He's the one who searches
all the books for more
designs: a pink brontosaurus grins
and hops, his Arapaho
eagle rises like fire, Norwegian
serpents curl
to bronze, aquamarine, and Spiderman
comes back again
and again without a sound
to my desk, to my lap—
the scraps, Manila, white
paper in sixteen folds.
And I'm the one
with the wide Caucasian face
who stares inscrutably
at the nets that bind. Down the hall
the soldiers' boys, pencils in fists,
grudge out the calligraphy of punishment—
I WILL NOT EXPLODE IN CLASS—
these sentences
knotting inside
one hundred times.

ROSEANN LLOYD

Remembering In Three Parts

1

When I remember I have no father
I want to cut off my hands. If I do
not have any hands, I do not have anything
to wring like a girl. If I am not
a girl, I cannot grow up
to be a woman. If I am
not a woman, I have no feelings
in my womanly parts and cannot touch
them with my hands. Neither can I
touch any other creature
with affection.

2

When I remember I have no father
I remember the nights I stayed up reading
to block out the pain and the psychologist
in the room next door pacing
his *sleep deficit*, hour after hour
of accumulating lack.
He said he'd never catch up. Even
in the winter the stand-up fan
beat itself across the floor. Once he
showed me how he shaved
his teddy bear. I tried to cover
my revulsion, said I had no problem
with mutilation. No problem with childhood
love, the deprivation thereof.

In this troubled extremity, my wrists
tingle. I say I must unhand
myself, curse the lack, walk
away. But the feet below
stumble on trouble, are troubled, can't
remember *left-right*
without their fellow hands

3

When I remember I have no father, I need
a laying on of hands, hands
that do not mind my phantom
pain, hands that touch
the centering parts, remembering me:
third-eye, nose, mouth, breast-
plate, belly
button, shining button.
Folded in
to this connection, mind, mine, I can unfold
and feel the length
of my extremities, the paradox of dualities,
how a body moves by twos—
arms, legs, centered-stretched,
loved-bereft, breasts,
my hands.

My hands, remembered now, remember
that they belong to me. They begin again
with useful work and love—
making patches, cooking stew, putting
things away. But they never
discover the place to hold
the words for *father*:
lack, deficit, deprivation of.

ROSEANN LLOYD

Tap Dancing For Big Mom

I'm sitting at the kitchen table, punching the color button of the oleo packet. It POPS like an egg but I can't feel the splatter in my fingers because the packet is thick as an innertube. I'm kneading the cold white dough inside until the orange marbles through it & it's not cold any more, now it's warm & the kitchen is sunny. Gramma is sitting next to me, pulling the feathers out of a chicken. The feathers are rusty in color. It's just me & her, sitting & talking. Nobody else is here. Of course there are other people in the house—there's Dora the Boarder who pours the water off the vegetables she cooks & saves it in the icebox in tall clear jars & drinks it later—Gramma says—for the vitamins, but I never get to see her do it so I don't know for sure if she does. There's Marlene who rents the apartment upstairs where Aunt Tid used to live. Tid is short for her real name Matilda, the baby sister of my great-gramma, Minnie Tennessee. Marlene can throw her voice into her dummy who is bigger than her baby & is the one I will think of years later every time I see Candace Bergen in a movie & feel sorry for her because of her sibling rivalry with a wooden boy. Marlene combs her hair so it looks like it is painted on her head like the dummy's. During the War she travelled all over the Pacific Theater entertaining our boys. The Pacific Theater is a stage with waves painted on the back-drop in navy blue. That dummy is somewhere in this house now and so is my brother who is probably crawling around under the dining room table where we play train, pretending the metal handles that open the table's middle for leaves are actually the controls to the train engine we drive through the back hills to smuggle supplies for Robert E. Lee or Ulysses S. Grant—we can't ever make up our minds which one it is because nobody will tell us who won the War Between the States & we won't even know that there's another name for the War until we move to Minnesota & even then I won't understand the Southern con-fusion of names because Gramma's hero is Abraham first Who Freed the Slaves and Ike second Who Loves His Wife, the one he is smiling at on the china plate on the wall. Gramma is my hero & she's the one I want to be with now, here in the kitchen, & there's nobody here but us, sitting & talking. And even if my memory is kind of funny, it's just like Gramma's, for she will later deny that she ever had to buy oly—not during the War or at any other time. She always puts butter on her table. But right now she is asking me how do I like coloring the oly & do I want to hear her story about how her daddy made her go to school when she was 5 years old & she had to sit in the seat at the front of the row without a desk & her feet dangled & didn't touch the floor & now it's my turn to tell a story & I'm talking like a really good tap dancer, fast at first, and then real slow, with easy, unexpected turns, & she never says, stop being silly, she never says, stop exaggerating, she never says, stop talking in your Bible voice. She says, yes, & then what happened? What happens next? Nothing happens next. I never have to leave this border state, she never has to die, we're here in the kitchen surrounded by sun & chicken feathers & she's saying, go on, Rosie, go on.

ROSEANN LLOYD

BARRY CASSELMAN was born in Erie, Pennsylvania. A poet, short story writer, and playwright, Casselman has had four books published, including two books of poetry: *A Rippling Water Sleeve* (Iowa City, 1979) and *Equilibrium Fingers* (Kraken Press, 1978). His poems have been published in a number of magazines and anthologies including *The Greenfield Review*, *Abraxas*, *Another Chicago Magazine*, *Kansas Quarterly*, *Medrona*, and *B-City*. His play, *A Huge Living Thing*, was performed recently by the Minnesota Orchestra at Sommerfest.

Casselman has been the editor and publisher of *Many Corners* newspaper for a number of years.

The Cold Is The Oldest Memory

The cold is the oldest memory:
cold wind and cold night.

The voice of the cold quiets whatever it touches,
whatever it reaches, and it forces us
to consider what a silence is, after all,
what our part of a silence is,
how lamentably we prepare for the cold seasons.

We make a provisional heat through each other,
through the nights we share in dark relief
from the impossible, illuminated days of our lives.

But the cold is no bully.
It means everything it says.

What is so warm about us
is the way we reappear in each other's lives,
even after we separate, even when we make journeys
that put each other far out of ourselves, even then,
even in our own desire, our tentatively touching each other,
our own unfathomable energy becomes a trace
that winds tortuously through our bodies, and leaves
a delicate scar on the membrane protecting us from the cold.

There is no respite from this.
The sun is only temporary heat.
The cold is much simpler than heat,
any heat we know.

The cold was the first warning.

Cold wind.
Cold night.
No stars.

BARRY CASSELMAN

Psalm Of Your Amino Anthems

Hey, if I said those words my words cover,
there would be words inside them, invisible bundles
of unvisited saluting properties.

Admit to it, and I mean you, especially me, as all of them,
we each want something partly, bodily, and more than we know
                                                        needing,
the geography of appetites, their fissures and bruises,
cuts, nipples and ordinary openings, in tempo, pressure.

You are now, I am saying, in the kitchen,
its acrobatic spins, its smells, liaisons;
you are then, I am saying, outside, a deep light you see
turned against a concrete building, a residence, the noise
of your feet walking on the street, hey,
keep up with this, I am saying I am doing.

This will go to there,
there saying at some time, ferns and laurel,
the skin of the face of one you desire, or any face;
a woman knows this, a man, glass windows in a large room,
boiled potatoes.

Now, let's talk about this in a way
of not talking about it, about talking,
as long as we're together, groaning and swelling,
words are part of it, not about it,
words are in it, not after it,
get it?

Wait for this.
You will have it.
Stout, whelming, palpable.
After words.
Groceries. Someone to talk to.

The incidental rescue of despair goes to the exact need,
the fertile lattice of the eyes looking through my eyes,
before words, before words.

The Gates Of Atonement Opening

A beautiful thing is unintentional;
we find it already being itself,
waiting for our admiration, waiting to spoil.

In my sleep, abandoned buildings appear in dark familiar
                                         neighborhoods,
brick warehouses made with brown and nostalgia,
the colors of pumpkins, sorrel, butter.

Make your defeats brief; your victories
full of stamina before you discard them.

The gates of the past are closed the moment we depart from any
                                             event,
which is the next moment, and place it deftly and partly into
                                             ourselves.

The nature of how we accumulate is a consecutive atonement,
absorbing words as our lives curve over the surfaces of the
                                           brown-red earth.

I see the past is a distracted pharaoh,
wrapped in generations of ribbons,
gripping a mandolin whose song is dry and silent.

Closing some gates leads to opening others,
like plasmas travelling by natural visa through your body,
like any reconciliation.

Think of a great stone bridge securely anchored in the open air.
If this is difficult, think instead of plain speech.

How is a chair like a door?
How like a curving fence is a feeling?

I observe an insolent convention of uncertainty.
I also notice how private thoughts come over you,
and perform small plays on your face.

Those gates are closed; they are closed, closed,
and you cannot think so much on that without losing your pace,
the strength you have.

And when I begin to worry about some thing,
I remember how unimportant the most important things are,

                        BARRY CASSELMAN

how precariously everyone moves through the world,
how steady is our obscurity
under the sun's imperious directions.

The mind does not weigh more than the world.

Those abandoned buildings reappear after sleep,
after our embraces, after conversations.
They come back into sight like wonders of the world,
colossal statuary in the deserted neighborhoods of the new cities,
cities bent into the earth like sticks in a garden.

Every day is a prayer we cannot speak aloud.
But we do utter it by lifting ourselves from our beds each

                                                    morning.
As if we were gates. As if we were gates.

A Cold Sea On The Moon

We have nearly covered the earth now
with our limitations,
our solemn ingenious self-portraits,
rich popular music,
and quarreling.

Early spring. Evening. A filigree
of infant leaves poking from branches
into the gray-orange sky.

Automobile sounds from the street.

To fall down properly, you lift up, too,
your weight waking going down.

This is a dance which leads us to our inconsiderable bodies.

But the world does not close like a store.

Then we seek unknown states of repetition;
surrogates for the panic in front of our dreams.
Constant and abundant messages come to us from other places.
Stars. Desperate bruises in the earth.

We pass each other politely near the street, don't we,
our voices full of exits.

The fragile conversations that cover us
covering this world.

You need to love your own work.

Past evening. Early spring. The dark sky
makes us listen carefully.

We pass each other near the street another time.
The dim light is a thin khaki tent over your loneliness.
Your eyes, moist and shaken.
You pause at the edge of speech
because you know your words will be like a cold sea on the
moon.

I want to tell you that we must get away from this for a while.
This world is so much more than we imagined.

BARRY CASSELMAN

Between night and morning. Early spring. Everyone is sleeping
in the seasonal coolness, a memoir of the bitterness behind us.
Mail trucks, flashing their headlights, bring in cargo
which covers the earth.

Only now, standing in the quieted street,
does the implacable world face me saying
"You are always naked, always mine, always a child."

We think we mean what we say.
We think we cover the earth.
We think we say no to each other.
We think we are alone.

Dear naked children.

JILL BRECKENRIDGE is the author of *Civil Blood*, poetry and prose about the U.S. Civil War (Milkweed Editions, 1986). Her sequence of eighteen poems titled *Gone with the West* was published in *Noeva: Three Women Poets* (Dakota Press, 1975). Her poems have appeared in such publications as *Poetry Now, 25 Minnesota Poets, Woman Poet: Midwest, Dacotah Territory*, and *Kansas Quarterly*. Breckenridge's work won both Loft-McKnight Awards (for Prose and Poetry) in 1985, a Bush Foundation Individual Artist Fellowship in 1980, and Minnesota State Arts Board grants in 1977 and 1983.

Currently, Breckenridge designs and teaches writing seminars to business and government agencies and works one-to-one with individuals on their writing. She has completed another book of poems and is at work on a novel.

Cabell

Moving from Virginia to Kentucky — Grandmother shows me a
letter sent to Grandfather from Colonel Thompson who took our
slaves to Kentucky and then hired them out: June 1792

Mister John Breckinridge, Virginia:
It is done, and not an hour too soon.
Approaching the River Monongahela, Red Stone
on its banks appeared a Second Eden —
our Whiskey, its blonde Mercy, had just
run dry. To tell the Truth, it got us there.
You know how they wailed when we left; it never ceased.
Six weeks, this trip, and four through mud
up to our knees, or snow and ice that froze
our hands and feet. I don't know what was worse,
flesh frozen or thawed with this result —
the soles of our feet peeled off in our hands
like bacon. I'm sorry to report we lost the wagon
in a slide that nearly claimed us all,
but Sam refused to let the horses go,
saved them both, the bay a little lame.
If I could name them, I'd call our Mountains Misery.
The Floods our first assault, every River
overflowed its banks to roughly claim
the neighboring house and field — trees sprouting
families, one a flock of hens and two cats.
(Is this the Fruit you speak of in Kentucky?)
We crossed a field, burned black except
for three spears, each waving a skull
like a white flag. Indians, we guessed,
Shawnee. We could not explain
the assemblage of small birds, blue and red,
circling the charred remains of the field, singing.
We had to chain the slaves from that day on.
Then the Mountains — and the rain, a River
pouring continuous night and day. Our canvas
tents bowed and poured on us like pitchers.
You know how slaves detest the high ground.
They dropped with every Thunder clap, thought
Lightning a lash splitting the Sky to face
them with their God — and this a furious fellow.

JILL BRECKENRIDGE

If it were not for Sam, his influence,
I would have lost them all at the final Summit.
Two men, I guess they were, freedmen,
though it was hard to tell, strung upside
down from the branch of a Poplar tree,
the feet gone, the heads too, and this
mutilation the last straw for the slaves, who fell
on the ground and would not move, prepared to die.
It was then I brought out our good friend, Whiskey,
gave them a shot every hour they weren't asleep,
and this way—some of them sick, some of them singing—
I brought them over the Mountains into Jordan.
They rested at Colonel Meredith's before we let
them out for hire. What a cry they put up!
to leave, a second time, their friends and relations.
Although we got less for the two old ones,
Sam and John brought Six Pounds, the childless
women, Three, women with children, Fifty
Shillings, and two boys at Eighteen apiece.
The Twenty Pounds of my advance covered
the journey's supplies. The trip itself demands
forgetting. I trust this letter finds you well.
Remaining yours, Sincerely, Colonel Thompson

Jacob

The Four Seasons: Harvest

Every slave shack's boasting strings
of shucky beans, red peppers,
run to jesus, shun the danger
I know the other world's not like this
and harvest corn, every rooftop's busy
drying peach and apple pies.
I won't stay much longer here
I know the other world's not like this
Old moon is full for the all night
corn shucking at Master Webb's,
run, sister, run, run, sister, run
I know the other world's not like this
a fire as high as a two-storied
house is burning red, then gold,
fire in the east, fire in the west
I know the other world's not like this
burning purple and blue. Faces
dancing wildly in the heat of flame,
you're going to reap just what you sow
I know the other world's not like this
alive with laughter, our songs of hope
sung out at the top of our lungs to the night,
I call myself a child of god
I know the other world's not like this
pig turning 'round on the spit,
shucked corn cool in your hands,
walk away, children, don't get weary
I know the other world's not like this
unless you find a red one—
then you get a swig of brandy,
up on the mountain, down in the valley
I know the other world's not like this
get to kiss any girl on the place.
I kiss Marcie, her skirt bulging
heaven is my rightful home
I know the other world's not like this
with pone cakes, dried apples, a blanket.
Tonight is the night we're going to run—

JILL BRECKENRIDGE

tell jesus done, done all I can
I know the other world's not like this
so when the moon helps us out,
hides its face behind a cloud,
slavery chains are broke at last
I know the other world's not like this
we crouch down, then run,
head north toward the wide Ohio and freedom.
a child of god, I'm on my way
I know the other world's not like this
Grampa Sam drew maps in the dirt
but night eats up remembering.
a long long time, I'm on my way
I know the other world's not like this
We run from bush to ditch to tree
singing softly to chase our fear.
my bones are aching, racked with pain
I know the other world's not like this
Twice, by full moon, I see
Sonny grinning his white grin.
I'm going to praise god till I die
I know the other world's not like this
Fire left behind, the hand of night
closes its fist around us.
meet me on that other shore
I know the other world's not like this

Will Sommers, Confederate Soldier

*December 30, 1862: The Night Before The Battle He Prepares
To Fight, Gun Not Loaded*

To have risen before the black rooster,
myself crowing in the new day, to have heard
the chorus of wild birds blessing the dew
on my land, to have sunk my hands up to the wrists
in dirt, dark and warm as inside of a cow,
reaching for the turned strangling head of her new one,
to have touched the silky tassel of wheat, golden,
the newly shorn rug of a sheep's back,
the white oak plank I've sanded smooth,
soft as the inside of a woman's elbow,
stroked the underwater skin of catfish, cool
and dark, that surprise of spines, to have dropped
seed into holes I alone made, firmed
warm earth down around them, to have witnessed
the first green shoots, threads of life
so strong in their push for sun they cracked
apart the earth, to have fought squirrel, crow,
rabbit, drought, army worm, drought,
weevil, flood, despair, Hessian fly,
grasshopper, blight, cankerworm, despair,
to keep new life alive, to have watched the green
blades of young corn curl under,
brown like brittle fodder in the scorch of sun,
to have mourned the hay rotting on the ground in rain,
to have held the still warm calf I could not save,
shot the delicate bay mare
mired in the mud hole, half eaten by wild boar,
to have smelled my wife's hair long
and darkly sweet, new washed, drying in the sun,
to have caught, with my rough hands, a daughter,
then two sons and held them, heard them, slippery
red, cry out their first hellos, to have built
a tiny box from the old cedar, buried a girl,
fist no bigger than a plum,
to have watched my wife's face, a full year
vacant as a winter pasture, to have smelled,
on the coldest day, the welcome warmth of urine and hay
from the just-opened barn door, returned

JILL BRECKENRIDGE

to the smell of coffee in the kitchen, fresh biscuit
and bacon, to have seen my wife's face slowly
brighten, her cheek regain its wild-rose blush
when I put my lips upon it, to have picked
and tasted the wild raspberry, sun-warmed,
sweet and sour as first dumb desire,
to have been partner with so much life,
to have lived this long, to have lived . . .

Tad Preston, Cadet

Quiet now . . . attack!

over the hard ground toward the stream where a hundred
artillery horses tied halter to halter lower their big
heads to drink, and I must shoot them, every one, kill the
dapple gray, who goes down on one knee, kill the bay, who,
mouth open, rears, black mane and tail flying, sprays blood
from its mouth in a final red flag, kill the chestnut who
stands perfectly still, insides trailing out behind, such
surprise in that look, shoot the black who rears, whinnies,
turning once around like a dancer, tips back into the stream
framed by foaming water, flying hooves and teeth and tails,
everything left alive screaming, everything dying, the dull
thunk after thunk of my bullets meeting solid flesh, and then
I take one down, blonde as my hair, step across its back,
so broad I lose my balance, sit down on its side as it raises
a heavy head, looks up at me with brown eyes, more than

human

in their trust, their questions I cannot answer, then one
breath heaved in and out, dies, this golden horse, gold of
wheat and summer sun, and just as I know there are angels,
I know the sky is daily stained with the cooled blood
of those who cannot speak for themselves

JILL BRECKENRIDGE

The South (IV)

The war, they say, is over.
Slave no longer,
the old carpenter, hands knotted,
is no less hungry.
When the scavengers rode off
with his daughter,
he heard her screaming his name
long after it
was silent. Then he got
a gun and bullets,
and with that gun, he shot
a rabbit, but found
no wood to cook it over.
War has eaten
every tree for miles around.
Muscle and bone,
his rabbit demands some
serious cooking.
He must chop up the birdhouse
that, years ago,
he built for his wife's wrens,
even the pole,
and as fire turns the rabbit
in the pot toward
tenderness, from the throat
of flame, he hears
the warbling song that seasoned
his May mornings.

Jill Breckenridge's poems are from *Civil Blood,* an epic of the Civil War era seen through the eyes of two protagonists, John Cabell Breckinridge [sic] and Jacob, his slave.

BILL HOLM was born in 1943 in Minneota, Minnesota, the grandson of Icelandic immigrant farmers. Though he has lived in the east, the west, in Iceland, in China, and even in St. Paul, his permanent address is still Minneota. His books are *Boxelder Bug Variations* (Milkweed Editions, 1985), *The Music of Failure* (Plains Press, 1985), *The Weavers* (Ox Head Press, 1985), *Minnesota Lutheran Handbook* (Westerheim Press, 1982), and *Warm Spell* (Westerheim Press, 1980). Holm is currently in central China, being, in his words, "a bourgeois liberal foreign expert."

Holm writes: "I regard Johann Sebastian Bach and Walt Whitman as the two primary reasons why the human race ought not to blow itself up: if we are lucky, they may happen again among us."

A Circle of Pitchforks

*A poem about the farmers' protest against a powerline
through Pope County, Minnesota.*

I

They used to call it a sheriff's sale.
Had one over by Scandia in the middle of the '30s.
My dad told me how
the sheriff would ride out to the farm
to auction off the farmer's goods for the bank.
All the neighbors would come with pitchforks
and gather in the yard—
"What am I bid for this cow?"
3¢. 4¢. No more bids.
If a stranger came in and bid a nickel
a circle of pitchforks gathered around him
and the bidding stopped.
Even in the grey light of memory
the windmill goes around uneasily.
The farmer's overalls
blow into the fork tines—
the striped overalls look like convict suits.
A smell of cowshit and wet hay seeps into everything.
The stranger wears tweed clothes
and a watch chain.
The sheriff's voice weakens
as he moves from hayrack to hayrack
holding up tools,
describing cattle and pigs
one at a time.

The space between those fork tines
is the air we all breathe.

II

"Resist much, obey little,"
Walt Whitman told us.
To bring light!
That's the thing!
Somewhere in North Dakota
lignite gouged out of the prairies

BILL HOLM

is transformed into light.
But you are not in darkness, brothers,
for day to surprise you like a thief.
We are all sons of light,
sons of the day;
we are not of the night,
or of darkness.
Let us not sleep, as others do
but keep awake and be sober.
Those who sleep,
sleep at night,
and those who get drunk,
are drunk at night.

III

There is so much light in Minnesota.
The white faces brought here from Arctic Europe,
the lines of white birch in the white snow,
white ice like a skin over the water,
even the pale sun seen through snow fog.
White churches, white steeples, white gravestones.

Come into an old café
in Ghent, or Fertile, or Holloway.
The air is steamy with cigarette smoke and frozen breath.
Collars up under a sea of hats pulled down,
you can hardly see the mouths moving under them.
The talk is low, not much laughing.
Eat some hot dish, some jello,
and have a little coffee and pie.
These are the men wrecking the ship of state —
The carriers of darkness.

Up in the cities
the freeway lights burn all night.

IV

My grandfather came out of Iceland
Where he took orders from the Danes and starved.

After he died, I found his homestead paper
signed by Teddy Roosevelt,
the red wax still clear and bright.
In the corner, a little drawing of a rising sun
and a farmer plowing his way toward it.
A quarter section, free and clear.
On his farm he found arrowheads
every time he turned the soil.
Free and clear. Out of Iceland.
In the thirties, the farm was eaten by a bank;
thrown back up when Olson
disobeyed the law that let them gorge.
In high school they teach
that Hubert Humphrey was a liberal
and Floyd Olson was a highway.

        V

Out on the power line barricades
the old farmers are afraid their cows'
teats will dry up after giving strange milk,
and their corn will hum in the granary all night.

They have no science, no words, no law,
no eminent domain
over this prairie full of arrowheads and flowers,
only they know it
and the state does not.

We homestead in our bodies too,
a few years, and then go back
in a circle
faster than the speed of light.

BILL HOLM

Poets and Scientists
Find Boxelder Bugs
Useful For Both
Metaphor and Experiment

Crush a boxelder bug.
After the little snap
a tiny liquid drop
the color of honey comes
out on your thumb.
The boxelder bug does not
hear this sound.
The red racing stripes on
his black back, like decorated
running shoes, finally don't
run anywhere, anymore.
You, on the other hand, have done
what your life prepared you for:
kill something useless and innocent,
and try to find some beauty in it.

The History of American Poetry, Or: Oscar Williams Looks at a Boxelder Bug for Readers' Digest Books

1

I think I could turn and live with the boxelder bugs.
They are so placid and self-contained.
I stand and look at them long and long.
Boxelder bugs bring me tokens of myself.
I wonder where did they get those tokens?
Did I pass that way huge times ago,
and negligently drop them?

2

So much depends upon a boxelder bug
covered with soap suds beside the white sink.

3

Whose bugs these are I do not know.
His tree is in the village though.
He will not mind me stopping here —
To scoop up bugs before the snow.

4

I was of three minds like a window
In which three boxelder bugs are crawling.
A man and a woman are one.
A man and a woman and a boxelder bug are one.

5

The bug comes in on little bug feet
sits looking over stove and icebox
on silent haunches and then crawls on

6

I, too, dislike them; there are things that are important beyond
    boxelder bugs.
Killing them, however, with a perfect contempt for them, one
    discovers something like affection for the little bastards —
imaginary windows with real boxelder bugs in them.

7

Fat black bugs in a wine barrel room
Barrel house bugs with wings unstable
Sagged and reeled and expired on the table
Boomlay, boomlay, boomlay, BOOM.

8

I thank you God for most this amazing
bug: for the crawling blackly spirits of trees
with a neat, sleek stripe of red, and for everything
which is unwanted, which is numerous, which is no.

9

I'd rather, except for the penalties, kill a man than a bug,
but the small black wing
had nothing left but a feeble wave which said, "Up yours."
I gave him the big thumb in the twilight

10

What happens to a bug in a window?
Does it dry up like a raisin in the sun
Or does it explode?
No. It eats in the kitchen and grows strong.

To Explain My Unusual Interest In
Boxelder Bugs, Particularly Those Who
Live In My Piano

I

I love whatever is difficult to kill:
Whales, grizzly bears, snapping turtles, boxelder bugs, some
    human beings,
Old Viking stories about corpses that won't stay dead.

I love stones that rest uneasy in the earth;
Boulders grunted up after the glacier;
Rock so anxious to see daylight, it bubbles out of volcano
    mouths.
I love water that freezes, takes a long time, and makes noises
Belching, snoring, moaning, sneezing, before spring melt.

I love old houses and barns that weather and lean into
    themselves.
You hear wind without opening the door.
The dresser leans forward.
Pictures slide to odd angles on the wall.
Weather comes, a guest, inside;
Still they refuse to fall unless
Beaten with crowbars and hammers.

II

You can kill anything by working at it;
The whole world of tame animals, dammed rivers,
Iron barns, tight houses, polished stones, helpful psychologists,
Heated pools, and half-dead people,
Wants you to join it,
Mails you invitations every day,
Each one more cordial and demanding.
Ignore them, and they grow hysterical, and will kill you.
Believe me, they can do it, and furthermore will be rewarded for
    it.
There is a bounty on *you*.

      BILL HOLM

III

I was one hundred years old the day I was born, and knew all
                                these things without words.
I felt it the first time I heard Beethoven played on a scratchy old
                                record player.
I felt it the first time I opened my eyes at a funeral and saw that
the corpse and I were the only two people alive in a
                                full church.
I felt it at eleven years old when I bought Walt Whitman's poems
                                for $3.50 in Sioux Falls.
I fingered the book for a long time, knowing inwardly someone
                                had come close.
I feel it now, early in the morning the way the *Art of Fugue*
                moves around under my fingers on an old piano.

IV

Most of all, I love an old piano that refuses to die,
To be thrown in the chicken coop, chopped apart with an ax;
A patient piano that develops a sense of humor after sixty years,
A few water marks, a few scratches, a clatter in the bushings as
                                felt
Hardens like an artery, a string going dead now and then.
This piano kept itself lean, doesn't eat much,
Its voice darkened and mellowed since 1922.
It plays noisy music quietly, quiet music like feathers dropped in
                                a well.
It's fit for Bach now, and music by old men.
It likes human beings and is kind to them,
Doesn't even mind boxelder bugs that live in it.
This piano will die, too, but not before saving many times the
                                odd man who plays it,
Sometimes gets out of bed late at night to feel its keys in the
                                dark.

Though We Flatter Ourselves As Individualists, There Is Always Another Part That Suspects The Contrary Truth

I

All alike, they disappear
into each other's lives,
without detection;
one wing black as the other,
each stripe red as the next.
Death doesn't happen
bug by bug,
but by season.

II

With us it's different, we think,
each raised to be odd,
the center of his own world,
without which nothing else is;
and it all goes down
with a burst of weeping,
a hollow space in the air
where our body stood.

III

Sometimes I long
to disappear, be one
of millions wearing
the same wings, crawling
in the same window, sitting
in a room full of others,
invisible, have them wonder what
was his name? No matter. . . .

BILL HOLM

Driving Past Westerheim Graveyard
(Jonina Sigurborg Josephson Holm
June 23, 1910–May 25, 1975)

You must be dry as a spring boxelder bug by now
In your underground house;
Nothing but bones and a husk.
The rest stands, like the bug,
Next to the coffee pot
Ready to tell stories.

You always knew it would happen this way.
Even when you are not in a room, you are
In it, your voice everywhere,
Under cushions, back of the stove,
Coming out from mouths of painted figurines.
Your breath still blows dust around
Under bric-a-brac.
Eyes on the pictures blink.

Each fall, new bugs crawl in,
Make pests of themselves again
In the same old way.
They look just like last year's batch.
Maybe they are.
I don't have to tell you these things.

DEBORAH KEENAN grew up in Bloomington, Minnesota. Her four published books are *Household Wounds* (New Rivers Press, 1981), *One Angel Then* (Midnight Paper Sales Press, 1981), *How We Missed Belgium*, written with poet Jim Moore (Milkweed Editions, 1984), and *The Only Window That Counts* (New Rivers Press, 1985). Keenan's work won her a 1986 Bush Foundation Individual Artist Fellowship and a 1987 NEA Fellowship. She is currently on the Core Faculty of The Loft and works as Managing Editor for Milkweed Editions.

Keenan lives in St. Paul with her husband, Stephen Seidel, and her three children, Brendan, Molly, and Joey.

Two Women

for jean adams

two women stepped away from two men, left for the country
where the snow was always clean, took their children for long
walks and wild rides down hills even ethan frome would have
thought twice about, dragged the children home on red and gold
sleds, and all the children got warm again in the bathtub while
the two women drank so much tea and hot chocolate in a blue
house it's a wonder they could ever fall asleep, except they were
tired from the walks and wild rides, from the long pull, their
children's bodies snow encrusted heavy jewels swaying behind
them, singing, "over the river and through the woods . . . " un-
til one woman laughed and one woman smiled, hearing the wild,
"hurrah for the pumpkin pie," for the twentieth time that day.

two women stepped away from two men, let the children run
wild new year's eve, wrapped them in their blankets, sang them
to sleep, made a fire, played cards, and there were no bets, and
nothing depended on either of them winning, and one woman
listened to rock and roll for the first time, and one woman wait-
ed for her favorite songs, hungry for benedictions. and the air
that night was not bitter, they fell asleep long before the bells
rang, long before the other children in the countryside took to
the streets, banging their mothers' pots and pans, celebratory
noise to honor a year no one felt safe making even one predic-
tion about, and the women made no resolutions, living weekend
to weekend as they did, nothing was resolved, although it was a
clear night, and the moon did its dance in the last december sky,
and the stars were in place and full of myth.

two women stepped away from each other, and the future hung like
twin stars, like a cold jewel between them, and one woman found
her way back to the man she loved, and the two children were happy
as they learned to reclaim the new version of an old life, and one
woman left for a new world, and two children learned to follow her,
knowing she would not let go of their hands.

two women left behind a blue house, where the air had always
been sculpted by women, left behind fists smashed onto tables,
and the idea of four children asleep in a room, black hair scat-
tered next to gold and brown, two women left behind the idea
of snow that one winter, that was always high and yielding, and
rows of snowsuits, endlessly drying on radiators, and one drove
away in a gold car, and one in a red car, back to an old city

DEBORAH KEENAN

where their futures unfolded like laundry every new day, where
all the white clothes slipped between their hands, reminding
them of clean snow, and children, and one woman kept cooking,
pots and pans scattered by a new baby, and one woman forgot
she knew how to cook anything, and all the children were smart
and beautiful and correct, and so were the two women.

Dialogue

I ask my mother to remember
the tennis courts   nets always
too high or sagging like old ones in the park

I asked my father about the sun
breaking on our backs as we struggled
to bring order to the wild raspberry patch

I asked a stranger on a country street
about Orion's belt   about his dagger
about winter's secret constellations

I asked my lover to notice the light
how it fills all second story windows   fills steeples
fills the white car at quarter to five in a winter afternoon

my mother takes that single memory
turns it to a recital of my childhood
clarified through the sieve of her watching eyes

my father   gone now and cold
answered   keep working
summer is brief here

the stranger said only that he liked stars
too shy to say more
an innocent in a world of dark

my lover listened said the light was Italian
had traveled here from Florence   said the light
was correct   that twilight was good
said he would not leave in twilight in winter in that light

there have been questions
I never knew there were answers to

there have been so many answers
they have all been right

DEBORAH KEENAN

Rock And Roll Destiny

> *I. We are not prisoners of rock and roll. We are volunteers.*
>
>   Peter Wolf, J. Geils Band

> *II. Badlands, you gotta live 'em everyday, let the broken hearts*
> *stand, it's the price you gotta pay . . .*
>
>   *Badlands*, Bruce Springsteen

> *III. With only you and what I've found, we'll wear the weary*
> *hours down.*
>
>   *Rose Darling*, Steely Dan

I.

They find each other accidentally. A turn of conversation, a line
from a rock and roll song slips from the other's mouth; suddenly
that mouth is desired. The sign, dead giveaway, one raw,
unyielding cynic left over from the sixties collides with another.
It won't be pretty but it won't be dull.

II.

It's not that simple. Never was. The badlands only a partial land-
scape, prisoners in some ways, they can never be sure whose
heart is breaking and whose is only bending. They both know
beginnings and endings are the only things that count in rock
and roll, and they've never been the types to figure out what
goes in between the passion and the swift fall from desire,
though they've done it over and over again. In rock and roll, do-
ing it more than once means little; you try not being a
professional about it but it comes naturally, with the territory.

III.

That's what they'd like it to mean sometimes. That continuity
might imply something besides boredom, submission to the ordi-
nary. The constant battle in the rock and roll heart, to seek, find,
hold dear, to recklessly change and mean it, to stop growing
smaller, less able to love. They've read too many books, watched
the hearts fall like snow, like a hand let go of, gracelessly drop-
ping to someone's side. They are volunteers, keep playing the
songs, let the tapes carry the dark, charged message of connec-
tion; somewhere inside themselves they agreed to live like this. It
works a few hours a week, they keep letting the music count, it's
a sin, a way to live.

The Amateur

Whenever a celebrated murder occurred Bolden was there at the
scene drawing amateur maps. There were his dreams of his
children dying. There were his dreams of his children dying.
There were his dreams of his children dying.
                    Coming Through Slaughter, Michael Ondaatje

In seventh grade geography we colored maps.
The continent of Africa was assigned when I
was in my red period. Each exotic country
challenged my crayons, my sense of harmony.
Cardinal red, plum, violet for the African
flowers on my mother's window ledge, wine,
the dark continent blossomed under my
steady left hand. Never before have so
many stars risen at the top of my work.
A true amateur, I colored for love.

An amateur parent at twenty-one, I was in
my blue period, to match my son's eyes and
the heaviness in my heart. His infant kabuki
hands defined the air, my dreams grew unsteady
as he grew more beautiful. I charted elaborate
plans for my life without him, while he dreamt
of clowns coming through the window to scratch
his eyes, and so we painted clowns, coloring
in details of anonymous faces, red stars on
flat white cheeks, blue triangles over empty
eyes. He slept easier then, while I dreamt
of masked men pushing him through the bedroom
window after disconnecting the stereo, severing
the telephone cord.

When my daughter in her dark beauty arrived,
I longed for hours of dream-filled sleep,
but she upset the mapping out I did for her
future with illness, her unsteady breathing
became the rhythm of my nights, for a year
all nights were broken, and she and I did
the rocking chair dance and far away in Africa
civil wars changed the names of half the countries
I had colored, believing they would never be altered.

DEBORAH KEENAN

It doesn't matter how many scientists explore
the country of sleep. It doesn't matter that
police draw white chalk lines around bodies
violently dispatched to eternity. Nothing
defines absence, there are no colors to choose
from when drawing in the shapes of missing
children, and when they slip away as you hold them,
or disappear under car wheels, or swim too far
in your dreams of water there are no rescues
plotted, the god of dreams is malevolent,
a professional, and you have done it all
for love, the competition is fixed, and the dream
of death is the first blossom after a child
blooms under your skin.

A Poem About White Flowers

my father chose a train
gave it the gift of his body
bright july sun
the engine lifted his form
hurled it   scattered it   moved on
we pretended there was enough left
to cremate

and the white flowers you gave me are so right
they fill my home
i think of them   slashes of petal white
i play endless game after endless loss
of solitaire
just so i can sit with those slashing white flowers
i love these flowers from you
they surprise me the way the roses didn't
they touch me the way a good white cliche
is supposed to touch all women who believe
in words like white and fragrance   who believe
in daisies pretending to be zinnias and in daisies
swearing they are white chrysanthemums

by the tracks my brother searched
for father's property
july sun burning to nothing the last
fragments of my father's beautiful
piano hands
he found the wallet   torn pictures
pieces of identity from a man
who came to dread his own

by the train station my brother found two lovers
who had been giving each other
their bodies
when they heard the train's emergency scream
they forgot the pleasure they had been seeking
and sought another
when they looked up the air carried
my father toward them   they were frightened
by the blood   the choice of death
so near their open fields of love

DEBORAH KEENAN

and the white flowers you gave me
don't fade today   the white
phosphorescent against a winter gray window
i love them for not fading today
for being white   not red   not dying   not red
for being white   and themselves
whatever they are   whatever they become

Greenland Mummy

The best preserved of all the Greenland mummies is the baby
boy mummy. He died quickly at six months of age, the snow his
bed, his blanket, his death. So intact, he takes the breath of the
archaeologists: two white shells — lower teeth, cornsilk for hair,
his tiny gloves, little blue starfish in the snow.

I make so much up. Haven't the time to study properly. I read
two pages, pronounce a novelist "psychotic." I read one paragraph and know more than I ever wanted to know about the
Greenland mummies.

The baby mummy was not wearing gloves; no shells, no cornsilk, a baby, not a doll. He was given to the snow after his
mother died, so he couldn't wear gloves or the beautiful red
overalls or the soft deerskin cap with ear flaps. I made all that up
when I was painting the baby mummy. I made it up so he would
be warm.

Given to the snow because his mother died. The old rules hurt,
not that the new rules are ideal. When the mother died in Greenland so many hundreds of years ago, then her baby was put
outside to die. And he became the best mummy, the one the
scientists love the best, because his little body froze so quickly,
more quickly than the grown-up mummies and the teen-age
mummies who died with their clothes on. It is good he froze so
quickly because the scientists are able to learn more from his tiny
body. It is good to freeze quickly when your mother dies. It is
good the rule was so clear: no aunts, no best friends of the
mother may take the child; it is good to sleep in the snow when
your mother dies. Maybe your aunt wouldn't love you enough,
maybe your mother's best friend would love her own baby
more. Who ever thought of such a dramatic rule in a country
named Greenland? Who thought of Greenland anyway, that
name of life, that huge island, and who thought of digging for
mummies in the first place?

I don't know these answers. I don't read much lately, except
what's assigned or what I struggle to see beyond a veil of tiredness. The baby wakes at night and I can't get back to sleep. I am
sitting outside his door, my back straight against the doorframe.
I am listening to each ragged breath he takes this month. I don't
read much because of the baby. The baby is why I make things
up. I love being up in the middle of the night with him; we
watch the news or old David Niven movies. We watched *Hawaii*,
we saw the circle of white, the halo/aura around Julie Andrews'

DEBORAH KEENAN

head after she screamed and pulled on the tied-in-knots bedsheet and had her first baby. That is the first scene I ever remember seeing of childbirth. Later, a baby is put into the beautiful ocean to drown. I turned the t.v. off then because Joey was falling asleep. I wouldn't have let him watch that scene anyway.

The snow is almost gone from our backyard. My daughter made a mermaid without a face, with purple yarn hair, only the hair and the last part of the flipping tail remain. My daughter wants to be a mermaid when she grows up. Our baby will never sleep in the snow. I won't even let him go winter camping, even if it's the only way he can win merit badges in Boy Scouts. The baby will keep his snuggie on, and his blue mittens from Aunt Peggy, and his dark blue snowsuit from Jean, and his Harlequin socks from Pat and Tim, and the baby will sleep indoors always unless we move to the tropics.

The Greenland baby mummy has a beautiful and haunting face. I keep thinking of him, his small face, how he would fit in the hands and arms and heart of his mother who died.

I have been in mourning for children all over the world since our baby was born six months ago. The news from China, Africa, Lebanon; you can't send money fast enough, you can't melt the snow fast enough, or turn down the sun, or grow the crops or stop the bombs fast enough. Our new baby has done his job well, the job all babies are assigned: he has broken open my heart for the third time in my life, he has made me think of all these babies, alive, dead and dying. This is the work of babies; that is why there is no time to read, why I make everything up as I go along.

They are searching for more Greenland mummies. The group graves are confusing to the archaeologists, so they hope to find more single graves. If they're lucky, they will stumble across another Greenland mummy baby. They hope the next one they find will have died even faster than the first. They long for what the snow does to babies.

That part may be wrong. They may have left Greenland by now. I will not be going to Greenland this year. I carry the picture of the baby mummy deep inside me, like something I swallowed that has nothing to do with food. One paragraph, one picture is enough. Our baby is sleeping right now. He is warm, getting over his ailments of the last month. He is the light in our house. Someday I will tell him all these stories, the sad ones, the famines, the girl children left out to die, and the happy ones, the mermaid in the backyard, the women who love him, the gifts they've given. I am glad winter is ending and that the snow is almost gone.

DEBORAH KEENAN

PHILIP DACEY was born in St. Louis, Missouri, in 1939. His books are *The Man with Red Suspenders* (Milkweed Editions, 1986), *Gerald Manley Hopkins Meets Walt Whitman in Heaven and Other Poems* (Penmaen Press, 1982), *The Boy Under the Bed* (Johns Hopkins University Press, 1981), and *How I Escaped from the Labyrinth and Other Poems* (Carnegie-Mellon University Press, 1977). His awards as poet include two NEA Fellowships, a Bush Foundation Individual Artist Fellowship, two Pushcart Prizes, a Discovery Award from the New York YM-YWHA's Poetry Center, a Loft-McKnight Award for Poetry, and a Woodrow Wilson Fellowship.

Dacey lives in southwestern Minnesota and has three children, Emmett, Austin, and Fay.

Edward Weston
In Mexico City

Clouds, torsos, shells, peppers, trees, rocks, smokestacks.
Let neither light nor shadow impose on these things
To give them a spurious brilliance or romance,
Let the mystery be the thing itself revealed
There for us to see better than we knew we could.
The pepper. The simple green pepper. Not so simple.
There are no two alike. Sonya brings me new peppers
Every day and each one leads me to the absolute
In its own way. My friends tell me the peppers
I've done cause physical pain and make
Beads of sweat pop out on the forehead. Orozco,
As soon as he saw them, said they were erotic.
I know nothing of that. I only know
Or seek to know the inner reality
Of each particular fruit, the secret
It tries but fails to hide because
In truth it would be known and taken;
The secret is of itself and beyond itself.
This pepper here: follow its form
And you enter an abstract world,
Yet always what you are making love to
Is pepper, pepper, pepper. It can both be
And not be itself.
                  The naked female body
When looked at in the right, that is the askew, way
Can also disappear while remaining fully
Present. Yesterday Tina was lying naked on the azotea
Taking a sun-bath. I was photographing clouds.
Then I noticed her and came down to earth
To shoot three dozen negatives in twenty minutes.
It was Tina I took, yet, in this picture,
Her right hip rises to become a slope
On the other side of Nature, and the ribs
The ribs are hesitancies, a fineness that will go
Only so far amidst the mass then wait
To be discovered by the quiet ones.
Tina, hello and goodbye, and hello.
Just don't ask me to make a formula of this.
With a formula I'd catch only the appearance

        PHILIP DACEY

Of a secret. But I must disappoint my friends
By always starting over again, day after day,
So that they say, "That's not a Weston, take it out!"
Unburdened of yesterday's victories. Today
It has been shells. Two shells, one a
Chambered Nautilus. I balanced them together,
One inside the other. White background, black background.
I even tried my rubber raincoat for a ground.
The shells would slip near to breaking.
I am near to breaking, too. That is my formula.
No, I break. I lose myself in the shells.

My friends are right, it's not a Weston, I'm gone,
Thank God. Gone into the luminous coils.
A coil's urge is to become a circle;
I'm what the coil needs to close the gap.
Pepper, torso, shell: they're circle, circle, circle.

And now for sleep. I'm going to look at the dark.
When I wake up, I won't know what I've seen
But I'll have seen it nevertheless. Tomorrow
I'll look at what's under the sun; if I see right,
I'll be remembering what I see tonight.

PHILIP DACEY

Owning A Wife

Who can own a woman
with brown stars on her back?

That cool expanse exceeds
whatever the measure says.

I peer close, a convert
to the new astronomy.

At the tip of one small finger
I have all these constellations.

But really I have none.
Nor, even, does the woman:

the stars belong as water
belongs in a clenched fist.

PHILIP DACEY

Sleeping Parents, Wakeful Children

When our parents were sleeping
We brought them gifts
It was a whispering time
The great bodies lain down
Upon the long bed
The deep sighs adrift
Through the upper rooms
It was a whispering time
When the gods slept
And we made gifts for them
With paints paper and tiny
Scissors safe for us
Masks and rings
Obscure magical things
In the halted hour
In the still afternoon
The anger asleep
And the jokes we didn't understand
The violent love
That carried our weather
All subsided to these
Two vulnerable ones
Their hands and mouths
Open like babes'
Their heads high
In the pillowy clouds
For all we knew dreaming us
Sneaking in
Lest they woke and discovered
Our love our fear
How we thrilled to appease
Praise and thank
Them in secret
My sister and I
Approaching the border
The edge of the platform
Where the gods murmured
So precise in our placement
Of these our constructions
Frivolous fair

The gifts on the skirts
Of their lives for surprise
Then turning away
Lips and fingers a cross
When they opened their eyes
They would never know how
When or why
They would never know
Who we were

PHILIP DACEY

Bourgeois Poem

This is not the bourgeois poem
you think it is. The father
is not a father
but the dictator of a small
Latin American country,
nor the mother a mother
but the peasantry the dictator
abuses. The children
are the land itself,
innocent, seasonal,
trampled upon
by the boots of the dictator's men,
watered
by the tears of the peasantry.
When milk spills
at the breakfast table,
blood runs
in the streets of the country.
When a door slams upstairs
between two faces,
men in suits and uniforms push away
from the opposite sides
of a long polished table and say
it is no use.

Right now someone
seems to be kissing
someone else in the poem,
but actually a young man
on a dusty road in that country,
coming upon his enemy,
has experienced a strange impulse
of good will. Something about the light,
perhaps, it is evening,
or the frayed shoes of the other.
The young man shoots, of course,
the impulse gets lost
in the habit of killing,
but not entirely, a colorful
bird, flushed by the shot,

rises from the nearby forest,
hovers, as if thinking
or being thought, then flies off,
trailing his impossible
tail-feathers. He looks like
the rainbow
a ray of light through a leaded-glass
window becomes
on a living-room floor.

PHILIP DACEY

The Reader At Midnight

for Pauline Chard on her 75th birthday

She reads late at night
while the others are sleeping.
It is her habit, her choice.

She has done this for years,
page after page,
to get the whole story

in lamplight, surrounded by dark,
by the sounds people make
as they fall into dreams.

The ghosts of the house gather round her,
whose hair is as white
as the page marked like years

and who's keeping this vigil
for sleepers, for stories,
for the heroes her novel invokes.

And she is the heroine here,
for a reader at midnight is central,
the world spins slowly around her:

should she nod, and she does,
a wheel tilts on its axis,
disturbing a sleeper

who struggles for balance
by dreaming of her,
this figure in lamplight,

this mother, this woman,
this reader of things.

Wild Pitches

You've been holding back
long enough, Son.
Stop aiming the ball.
Let your power,
that animal,
out. Don't worry
about hurting me.
I'm in my father-squat
behind homeplate, like a frog,
the soon-to-be-a-prince frog,
nothing and nobody
can stop that story.
Not even you. The whole world
squats so, just waiting
for you to throw the ball
as if you meant it,
an angry word,
an idea
to change the world,
a declaration
of love. It's true
some pitches will go wild.
At first a lot will.
But remember,
God is somewhere
with a mask and protector
for his chest and nuts
and catches every
wild pitch there is.
He's a scrambler.
So let that arm uncurl
and snake out
like the snake that girdles
the world—whip-snake,
diamonded and poisoned
to the point where
the wildest pitch
is the one that stays
in your hand.

PHILIP DACEY

PHEBE HANSON'S first book, *Sacred Hearts*, was published by Milkweed Editions in 1985. Her work has been widely published—in *25 Minnesota Poets, Poets of Southwestern Minnesota, Women Poets of the Twin Cities, WARM Journal, Woman Poet: Midwest, Saturday's Women*. Hanson's work won her a Bush Foundation Individual Artist Fellowship in 1985, and she took a year's leave of absence from teaching to live in Montevideo, Minnesota, and to work on a new manuscript.

Hanson writes: "The gift of a little blue five-year diary when I was ten began my writing career. Obedient child that I was, I began filling up those lined pages after reading the injunction inside the book: *Memory is elusive—capture it!* I've been keeping journals steadily since then."

First Car

Here he is in an old photo album,
my Norwegian immigrant father,
newly-ordained graduate of Augsburg Seminary.·
My first car—1926,
he has written under the boxy Model T,
familiar car like a child's drawing,
home-made looking,
a car so simple even a child
could drive it,
and I used to pretend,
perched on Daddy's lap,
while we sat in the driveway
waiting for Mother.
Darling and doted-upon first child,
I was stuffed into elaborate costumes,
hair curled and beribboned,
safe in the front seat
between Mother and Daddy,
who drove us to his churches in the country,
Camp Release and Black Oak Lake.
We sang together on the way,
I'll be a sunbeam for Jesus,
I'll shine for Him each day,
In every way try to please Him,
At home and school and play,
that winter night, bitter cold,
snow hissing against our windshield,
the only car out in the midnight storm.
Our dashboard burst into flame;
Daddy disturbed my cozy sleep
against Mother's arm
to rush us out of the car
to stand on the shoulder, hoping
for someone to stop.
That image of the three of us remains,
minister father in long black coat,
mother with fur collar surrounding her face,
child in blue snowsuit and aviator helmet,
as if we were posing for a studio portrait,
as if the swirling snow and relentless wind

PHEBE HANSON

were fake backdrops in those old photographs
where the faces radiate a strange silvery light,
and the eyes seem to know that death's ahead
from tuberculosis, pneumonia, diphtheria.
We still stand in the bright blizzard light,
frozen images by the side of the road.
I don't remember what happened next.
I don't remember ever being rescued.

Mother

We listened to strange lullabies
when we were young, sung by our
mother as she lay in her coffin
in our living room. When they
came to move her to the cemetery,
she announced they were not going
to bury her yet, that we must first
learn to honor her dead as we had
learned to honor her alive. Every
morning she sat bolt upright in her
casket by the piano and spoke out
the day's commands. We listened
with respect to her terse words.
It is not easy for the dead to
speak. They are not allowed
to say much, and they must make
every word count. Whatever she
told us we did, because the words
did not come lightly from her tongue.
She had grown less lenient in death,
made only bony demands now, and we
felt the rigor of her presence
until we entered high school and
moved away to the city, leaving her
coffin behind, alone in the empty house.

PHEBE HANSON

Curls

They told me,
the women who came
bearing macaroni hot dishes:
You must look nice
for the funeral.
They took out the long
curling iron, plugged
its cobra-skinned cord
into our current,
rolled heavy straight strands
around the hot cylinder's mouth
until my long hair
sprang out alive and curly,
frantic corkscrews bobbing
on my puffed sleeves.
But I pulled away
from their soft hands,
ran from them to the sink,
poured palmfuls of cold water
through my curls until they hung
on my neck and I was plain enough
to bend and kiss my mother's hard lips
as she lay in her coffin.

The Wrestler

My father retired early from the Lutheran ministry, & he had
plenty of time on his hands, only 62 years old, with stored-up
energy from sitting at a desk for so long, writing sermons, so he
began to fix up his house in Highland Park, St. Paul, turning the
basement into a one-bedroom apartment complete with fully-
functioning fireplace, although he always got rather testy when
he discovered his tenants actually used it, something he *never* did
with the fireplace in his living room, preferring to keep it always
smoke and ash free, and he made the attic over into a snug
efficiency, providing tidy rental income for himself and my step-
mother in their declining years, but he was not really declining,
still did supply preaching often in churches around the city, and
always taperecorded his sermons so he could present the cassettes
to me at Christmas or force me into his study when I came over
to visit to sit and listen to them, over my objections: "I'd rather
talk to you, Dad, than listen to these tapes of your sermons,"
wanting to add, but never doing it, "Heard one of them, you've
heard them all," and he also took to watching professional wres-
tling on television, that mammoth Curtis Mathis console that
dominated his living room. How strange to see him absorbed in
those moving pictures, he who had denied me the pleasures of
movies in my childhood, inveighing against the immorality of
Hollywood movie stars, their carnality and riotous living, how
strange to watch him now devour the sight of all that wrestling
male flesh. So today when I am shopping in Gary's Red Owl—
even the impersonal chains are made to feel humanly-owned here
in Montevideo, Minnesota, mobile home capital of our state, as
the sign proclaims when you enter from the east—I wheel my
cart slowly down every aisle, on a desultory quest for groceries I
don't really need, & my heart is suddenly gladdened by the sight
of a bright red folder in the school supply section, titled THE
HULKSTER and picturing the massive shoulders and torso,
bronzed and oiled, of the World's Heavyweight Wrestling
Champion, his enormous trophy held so as to mostly cover the
tight electric-blue stretch trunks he's poured into, and I buy the
folder for you, father, whose flesh must by now be almost gone
inside that casket we picked for you six years ago when the
funeral director said of the one we had chosen because as you
had instructed us it was the cheapest, "That one may be too small
for Reverend Dale. He was a husky man, you know. His shoul-
ders were very broad," and I realized almost for the first time,
father, you had a body made of flesh and blood, a body built like
a wrestler's.

PHEBE HANSON

Rumble Seat

Yesterday in the antique store
I walked into a pale peach chiffon dress,
like the one Darlene Oakwig wore
for her confirmation in 1935,
an antique dress now, but brand new then
and store-bought with cape sleeves, bias cut,
draped softly over her white arms,
skirt with scalloped hem that dipped
and rose against her slender legs
in silk stockings for the first time.
She lives still in my father's attic
where the pictures from his confirmation classes
lie stacked next to his old theology books.
This morning she calls to me from behind
the wet stones of the old houses I pass
on my morning walk down Summit Avenue,
her hair in soft waves,
finger waves we called them,
framed by fingers dipped in thick clear lotion.
My girl friends and I yearned to know how
to do it, envied the older girls like Darlene
with curves of hair swooping down around
her bland impassive face in the confirmation picture,
her eyes movie-star languid, her mouth impatient.
I watched her from afar, a child mild and obedient,
and later I heard the grownups whisper how she
had grown wild, like the wildness of my own daughter at sixteen
going out with the twenty-seven-year-old punk rock singer.
Darlene Oakwig rode in rumble seats with boys
from Hector and Clarkfield, towns only a few miles
down the road from Sacred Heart, but foreign and strange
to us, dark with mystery and wickedness.
She rode away from her confirmation vows
to renounce the Devil and all his works and ways,
rode away to drink beer and laugh loudly with rough, older
                                                    boys
in rumble seats, uncovered passenger seats that opened
out from the rear of their cars, not family cars
with safely-enclosed back seats, but wild roughneck cars,

open to the wind, gravel spitting into their laughing mouths.
Darlene Oakwig, killed in a car crash coming home
from a dance in Hector, her gravestone next to our family's
in the little cemetery on the outskirts of town,
Darlene Oakwig, far older than me, her eyes
in the confirmation picture already seeing
what I have not yet looked upon.

PHEBE HANSON

Prayer Meeting

There is a fountain filled with blood,
Drawn from Emmanuel's veins,
And sinners plunged beneath that flood,
Lose all their guilty stains.

We sing sitting in a circle on folding chairs
at Wednesday night prayer meeting where fourteen women
have gathered to pray and testify with my minister father.
There is one other man, too old and crazy to be counted,
who jumps up from time to time and shouts:
I'm just an old sinner, saved by grace!
He sneaks me always a hard white peppermint
from a dirty, crushed brown paper bag.
Surely tonight the powerful mint will strengthen
my mouth when it is my turn to speak out for the Lord.
Surely tonight I will not disappoint them.

When the singing is over and it is time to pray,
we drop to our knees in front of our chairs,
folded hands pressed against our bowed heads.
There are prayers as always for me, the little sister
in our midst, a stubborn and difficult child, motherless.
Only the Lord can save her, make her His true child,
if she will repent and forsake her willful ways.

The peppermint grows stronger as it dissolves
like a thick communion wafer on my trembling tongue.
Soon it will be my turn, I who have said nothing
after they have prayed for me week after week.
Some have even cried, remembering the day
my dear mother went home to be with Jesus.

I open my eyes, see through my intertwined fingers
only the eyes of my father, open, looking
at me, waiting for me to speak at last.
I hear my shaky voice rise faint and unfamiliar.
I am saying I hope Jesus will forgive me for
all the bad things I have done and all the times

I fought with my brother when my mother was sick
and trying to rest and how instead she got sicker
and then she died even though I prayed and promised

never to be bad again if Jesus wouldn't take her
away to be with Him in heaven.

Now I am sobbing and shaking, and all the women
rush over to touch me and cry: *Praise Jesus!*
He has saved our little sister tonight! Praise Jesus!

The peppermint man reaches into his pocket,
looks away as he hands me the candy.

PHEBE HANSON

I Listen To The Radio In Montevideo, Minnesota
And Think Of My Son Who Will Soon Be Thirty

Someone, it's Lois, I think, is interviewing the
new city manager, who's been here since October,
he's young, not even thirty, I guess, since he
informs us he graduated from college in 1980,
and he has a career plan and tells about it in
a quiet, totally confident monotone, how after
he's been a city manager for five years in a
small Ohio town, he decides it would be good for
his career plan to apply for the Montevideo job,
because he feels a new location would be a challenge,
and he's delighted to find he's one of the finalists,
and even more pleased at the news he's been selected
for this new opportunity which fits in so nicely
with his career plan and he says he's now exactly
at the stage in his career plan he wants to be, and
I think of my own son, who will be thirty next month,
who has never discussed with me his career plan,
beyond his desire to continue as an anarchist, working
in a collectively-owned vegetarian restaurant on the
west bank of the university campus, tie-dyeing t-shirts
in gaudy and joyful colors in his backyard on summer
afternoons and raising with his serene and intelligent
wife my perfect granddaughter, and as I lie here
recovering from a brutal and relentless flu, as radio
voices float over and around my dozing body, a memory
rises, of my son the spring he was three, how he danced
the Horah at Temple Israel Nursery School, where he went
for two years until he almost forgot he was Lutheran,
persuading me at Purim to make Hamantoshen pastries for
him and his nursery school buddies, how as he danced
in his short grey wool pants held up by suspenders over
the white cotton shirt I'd sewn for him from a Simplicity
pattern, the suspenders broke and his pants started to
fall down around his fat bare legs, but he didn't seem
to care, just kept leaping up and down to the wild ecstatic
music, while he held his pants up with one of his hands,
and never once stopped dancing.

Santa Lucia

December, 1938
and my grandparents
give their yearly party
at the church where
my grandfather is janitor.
Everyone comes to honor
Lucia, strange saint
for Swedes, virgin & martyr
of Syracuse, whose fiancé
denounced her
when she became a Christian
ordered boiling oil
and burning pitch
poured over her
stubborn head,
but on this night
I am 10,
know nothing
of that other Lucia,
know only I
get to put on the long white choir robe
tied with red satin sash,
get to wear the crown of candles
that remind everyone
of the light she brought
when she appeared
to Swedish peasants
during a famine.
I am afraid
as Grandma lights
the candles
in the crown on my head,
that the flames
will catch my hair on fire,
but I walk in slowly
head held straight,
carrying a tray of *lussekatter*
and deliver pieces of the bread
to all the Swedes
gathered in Gloria Dei Lutheran Church

PHEBE HANSON

that long-ago December night
just before the world
burst into flames.

ROBERT BLY was born in Minnesota in 1926. His first book, *Silence in the Snowy Fields*, was published in 1962, and four years later he founded, with David Ray, American Writers Against the Vietnam War. His second book, *The Light Around the Body*, was published in 1967 and received The National Book Award that year. Since then he has published *The Morning Glory*, *Sleepers Joining Hands*, *This Tree Will Be Here for a Thousand Year*, *This Body Is Made of Camphor and Gopherwood*, *The Man in the Black Coat Turns* and *Selected Poems*. He has also published ten books of translations. The University of Michigan Press published a book of interviews with Bly called *Talking All Morning* and the Sierra Club published an anthology edited by Bly titled *News of the Universe*.

Robert Bly and his wife live in Moose Lake, Minnesota.

Awakening

We are approaching sleep: the chestnut blossoms in the mind
Mingle with thoughts of pain
And the long roots of barley, bitterness
As of the oak roots staining the waters dark
In Louisiana, the wet streets soaked with rain
And sodden blossoms, out of this
We have come, a tunnel softly hurtling into darkness.

The storm is coming. The small farmhouse in Minnesota
Is hardly strong enough for the storm.
Darkness, darkness in grass, darkness in trees.
Even the water in wells trembles.
Bodies give off darkness, and chrysanthemums
Are dark, and horses, who are bearing great loads of hay
To the deep barns where the dark air is moving from corners.

Lincoln's statue, and the traffic. From the long past
Into the long present,
A bird, forgotten in these pressures, warbling,
As the great wheel turns around, grinding
The living in water.
Washing, continual washing, in water now stained
With blossoms and rotting logs,
Cries, half muffled, from beneath the earth, the living
    awakened at last like the dead.

ROBERT BLY

A Dream Of Retarded Children

That afternoon I had been fishing alone,
Strong wind, some water slopping in the back of the boat.
I was far from home.
Later I woke several times hearing geese.
I dreamt I saw retarded children playing, and one came near,
And her teacher, face open, hair light.
For the first time I forgot my distance;
I took her in my arms and held her.

Waking up, I felt how alone I was.
I walked on the dock,
Fishing alone in the far north.

After Drinking All Night With A Friend, We Go Out In A Boat At Dawn To See Who Can Write The Best Poem

These pines, these fall oaks, these rocks,
This water dark and touched by wind—
I am like you, you dark boat,
Drifting over water fed by cool springs.

Beneath the waters, since I was a boy,
I have dreamt of strange and dark treasures,
Not of gold, or strange stones, but the true
Gift, beneath the pale lakes of Minnesota.

This morning also, drifting in the dawn wind,
I sense my hands, and my shoes, and this ink—
Drifting, as all of the body drifts,
Above the clouds of the flesh and the stone.

A few friendships, a few dawns, a few glimpses of grass,
A few oars weathered by the snow and the heat,
So we drift toward shore, over cold waters,
No longer caring if we drift or go straight.

ROBERT BLY

The Dead Seal

I

Walking north toward the point, I come on a dead seal. From a
few feet away, he looks like a brown log. The body is on its
back, dead only a few hours. I stand and look at him. There's a
quiver in the dead flesh: My God, he's still alive. And a shock
goes through me, as if a wall of my room had fallen away.

His head is arched back, the small eyes closed; the whiskers
sometimes rise and fall. He is dying. This is the oil. Here on its
back is the oil that heats our houses so efficiently. Wind blows
fine sand back toward the ocean. The flipper near me lies folded
over the stomach, looking like an unfinished arm, lightly glazed
with sand at the edges. The other flipper lies half underneath.
And the seal's skin looks like an old overcoat, scratched here and
there—by sharp mussel shells maybe.

I reach out and touch him. Suddenly he rears up, turns over. He
gives three cries: Awaark! Awaark! Awaark!—like the cries from
Christmas toys. He lunges toward me; I am terrified and leap
back, though I know there can be no teeth in that jaw. He starts
flopping toward the sea. But he falls over, on his face. He does
not *want* to go back to the sea. He looks up at the sky, and he
looks like an old lady who has lost her hair. He puts his chin
back down on the sand, rearranges his flippers, and waits for me
to go. I go.

2

The next day I go back to say goodbye. He's dead now. But he's
not. He's a quarter mile farther up the shore. Today he is thinner,
squatting on his stomach, head out. The ribs show more: each
vertebra on the back under the coat is visible, shiny. He breathes
in and out.

A wave comes in, touches his nose. He turns and looks at me—
the eyes slanted; the crown of his head looks like a boy's leather
jacket bending over some bicycle bars. He is taking a long time
to die. The whiskers white as porcupine quills, the forehead
slopes. . . . Goodbye, brother; die in the sound of waves. For-
give us if we have killed you. Long live your race, your
inner-tube race, so uncomfortable on land, so comfortable in the

ocean. Be comfortable in death then, when the sand will be out of your nostrils, and you can swim in long loops through the pure death, ducking under as assassinations break above .you. You don't want to be touched by me. I climb the cliff and go home the other way.

ROBERT BLY

Counting Small-Boned Bodies

Let's count the bodies over again.

If we could only make the bodies smaller,
the size of skulls,
we could make a whole plain white with skulls in the moonlight.

If we could only make the bodies smaller,
maybe we could fit
a whole year's kill in front of us on a desk.

If we could only make the bodies smaller,
we could fit
a body into a finger ring, for a keepsake forever.

For My Son Noah, Ten Years Old

Night and day arrive, and day after day goes by,
and what is old remains old, and what is young remains young
and grows old.
The lumber pile does not grow younger, nor the two-by-fours
lose their darkness;
but the old tree goes on, the barn stands without help so many
years;
the advocate of darkness and night is not lost.

The horse steps up, swings on one leg, turns his body;
the chicken flapping claws up onto the roost, its wings whelping
and walloping,
But what is primitive is not to be shot out into the night and the
dark,
and slowly the kind man comes closer, loses his rage, sits down
at table.

So I am proud only of those days that pass in undivided
tenderness,
when you sit drawing, or making books, stapled, with messages
to the world.
or coloring a man with fire coming out of his hair.
Or we sit at a table, with small tea carefully poured.
So we pass our time together, calm and delighted.

In Rainy September

In rainy September, when leaves grow down to the dark,
I put my forehead down to the damp, seaweed-smelling sand.
The time has come. I have put off choosing for years,
perhaps whole lives. The fern has no choice but to live;
for this crime it receives earth, water, and night.

We close the door. "I have no claim on you."
Dusk comes. "The love I have had with you is enough."
We know we could live apart from one another.
The sheldrake floats apart from the flock.
The oak tree puts out leaves alone on the lonely hillside.

Men and women before us have accomplished this.
I would see you, and you me, once a year.
We would be two kernels, and not be planted.
We stay in the room, door closed, lights out.
I weep with you without shame and without honor.

Listening To The Köln Concert

After we had loved each other intently,
we heard notes tumbling together,
in late winter, and we heard ice
falling from the ends of twigs.

The notes abandon so much as they move.
They are the food not eaten, the comfort
not taken, the lies not spoken.
The music is my attention to you.

And when the music came again,
later in the day, I saw tears in your eyes.
I saw you turn your face away
so that the others would not see.

When men and women come together,
how much they have to abandon! Wrens
make their nests of fancy threads
and string ends, animals

abandon all their money each year.
What is that men and women leave?
Harder than wrens' doing, they have
to abandon their longing for the perfect.

The inner nest not made by instinct
will never be quite round,
and each has to enter the nest
made by the other imperfect bird.

ROBERT BLY

The Hockey Poem
for Bill Duffy

1. The Goalie

The Boston College team has gold helmets, under which the long black hair of the Roman centurion curls out. . . . . And they begin. How weird the goalies look with their African masks! The goalie is so lonely anyway, guarding a basket with nothing in it, his wide lower legs wide as ducks'. . . . . No matter what gift he is given, he always rejects it. . . . He has a number like 1, a name like Mrazek, sometimes wobbling his legs waiting for the puck, or curling up like a baby in the womb to hold it, staying a second too long on the ice.

The goalie has gone out to mid-ice, and now he sails sadly back to his own box, slowly; he looks prehistoric with his rhinoceros legs; he looks as if he's going to become extinct, and he's just taking his time. . . .

When the players are at the other end, he begins sadly sweeping the ice in front of his house; he is the old witch in the woods, waiting for the children to come home.

2. The Attack

They all come hurrying back toward us, suddenly, knees dipping like oil wells; they rush toward us wildly, fins waving, they are pike swimming toward us, their gill fins expanding like the breasts of opera singers; no, they are twelve hands practicing penmanship on the same piece of paper. . . . They flee down the court toward us like birds, swirling two and two, hawks hurrying for the mouse, hurrying down wind valleys, swirling back and forth like amoebae on the pale slide, as they sail in the absolute freedom of water and the body, untroubled by the troubled mind, only the body, with wings as if there were no grave, no gravity, only the birds sailing over the cottage far in the deep woods. . . .

Now the goalie is desperate . . . he looks wildly over his left shoulder, rushing toward the other side of his cave, like a mother hawk whose chicks are being taken by two snakes . . .
suddenly he flops on the ice like a man trying to cover a whole double bed. He has the puck. He stands up, turns to his right, and drops it on the ice at the right moment; he saves it for one of his children, a mother hen picking up a seed and then dropping it. . . .

But the men are all too clumsy, they can't keep track of the puck . . . no, it is the *puck*, the puck is too fast, too fast for human beings, it humiliates them. The players are like country boys at the fair watching the con man — the puck always turns up under the wrong walnut shell. . . .

They come down ice again, one man guiding the puck this time . . . and Ledingham comes down beautifully, like the canoe through white water, or the lover going upstream, every stroke right, like the stallion galloping up the valley surrounded by his mares and colts, how beautiful, like the body and soul crossing in a poem. . . .

3. *Trouble*

The player in position pauses, aims, pauses, cracks his stick on the ice, and a cry as the puck goes in! The goalie stands up disgusted, and throws the puck out. . . .

The player with a broken stick hovers near the cage. When the play shifts, he skates over to his locked-in teammates, who look like a nest of bristling owls, owl babies, and they hold out a stick to him. . . .

Then the players crash together, their hockey sticks raised like lobster claws. They fight with slow motions, as if undersea . . . they are fighting over some tribal insult or a god, but like lobsters they forget what they're battling for; the clack of the armor plate distracts them and they feel a pure rage.

Or a fighter sails over to the penalty box, where ten-year-old boys wait, to sit with the criminal, who is their hero. . . . They know society is wrong, the wardens are wrong, the judges hate individuality. . . .

4. *The Goalie*

And this man with his peaked mask, with slits, how fantastic he is, like a white insect, who has given up on evolution in this life; his family hopes to evolve after death, in the grave. He is ominous as a Dark Ages knight . . . the Black Prince. His enemies defeated him in the day, but every one of them died in their beds that night. . . . At his father's funeral, he carried his own head under his arm.

ROBERT BLY

He is the old woman in the shoe, whose house is never clean, no matter what she does. Perhaps this goalie is not a man at all, but a woman, all women; in her cage everything disappears in the end; we all long for it. All these movements on the ice will end, the advertisements come down, the stadium walls bare. . . .
This goalie with his mask is a woman weeping over the children of men, that are cut down like grass, gulls that stand with cold feet on the ice. . . . And at the end, she is still waiting, brushing away the leaves, waiting for the new children developed by speed, by war. . . .

My Father's Wedding
1924

Today, lonely for my father, I saw
a log, or branch,
long, bent, ragged, bark gone.
I felt lonely for my father when I saw it.
It was the log
that lay near my uncle's old milk wagon.

Some men live with an invisible limp,
stagger, or drag
a leg. Their sons are often angry.
Only recently I thought:
Doing what you want . . .
Is that like limping? Tracks of it show in sand.

Have you seen those giant bird-
men of Bhutan?
Men in bird masks, with pig noses, dancing,
teeth like a dog's, sometimes
dancing on one bad leg!
They do what they want, the dog's teeth say that!

But I grew up without dogs' teeth,
showed a whole body,
left only clear tracks in sand.
I learned to walk swiftly, easily,
no trace of a limp.
I even leaped a little. Guess where my defect is!

Then what? If a man, cautious
hides his limp,
somebody has to limp it! Things
do it; the surroundings limp.
House walls get scars,
the car breaks down; matter, in drudgery, takes it up.

On my father's wedding day,
no one was there
to hold him. Noble loneliness
held him. Since he never asked for pity
his friends thought he
was whole. Walking alone, he could carry it.

ROBERT BLY

He came in limping. It was a simple
wedding, three
or four people. The man in black,
lifting the book, called for order.
And the invisible bride
stepped forward, before his own bride.

He married the invisible bride, not his own.
In her left
breast she carried the three drops
that wound and kill. He already had
his barklike skin then,
made rough especially to repel the sympathy

he longed for, didn't need, and wouldn't accept.
They stopped. So
the words are read. The man in black
speaks the sentence. When the service
is over, I hold him
in my arms for the first time and the last.

After that he was alone
and I was alone.
No friends came; he invited none.
His two-story house he turned
into a forest,
where both he and I are the hunters.

When The Dumb Speak

There is a joyful night in which we lose
Everything, and drift
Like a radish
Rising and falling, and the ocean
At last throws us into the ocean,
And on the water we are sinking
As if floating on darkness.
The body raging
And driving itself, disappearing in smoke,
Walks in large cities late at night,
Or reading the Bible in Christian Science windows,
Or reading a history of Bougainville.
Then the images appear:
Images of death,
Images of the body shaken in the grave,
And the graves filled with seawater;
Fires in the sea,
The ships smoldering like bodies,
Images of wasted life,
Life lost, imagination ruined,
The house fallen,
The gold sticks broken,
Then shall the talkative be silent,
And the dumb shall speak.

ROBERT BLY

Jim Moore has published two books of poetry, *The New Body* and *What the Bird Sees* (University of Pittsburgh Press), and a collaborative book of poems, *How We Missed Belgium,* with Deborah Keenan (Milkweed Editions). His poems have appeared in *The Nation, The Paris Review, The Kenyon Review, American Poetry Review,* and others. He has received Minnesota State Arts Board and Loft-McKnight awards, and a Bush Foundation Individual Artist Fellowship. He teaches writing and literature at the Minneapolis College of Art and Design.

Cary Waterman is the author of three books of poems: *First Thaw* (Minnesota Writers' Publishing House); *The Salamander Migration* (University of Pittsburgh Press); and *Dark Lights the Tiger's Tail,* co-authored with her daughter, Amy (Scopcraeft Press). She has been awarded two Bush Foundation Fellowships and a recent Minnesota State Arts Board Fellowship. Her work has appeared in several anthologies and in a number of journals. She is currently on the faculty of Mankato State University.